Dear Leah,

מזל טוב on your בת מצוה.

You're a wonderful girl, and

you should continue to grow

in תורה and מצות

and bring lots of נחת to

your parents!

באהבה רבה

אודי ורבקה

To our dear המאושרת

לאה בת מזל,

May you continue to draw inspiration

in your life as a בת מצוה from

our beautiful evening tonight, and

from the saintly subject of this

book ... And may we in פ״ס יפיקו

always have tremendous אויבער נחת

from you -- תמיד!

With love,

אודי ורבקה בלוך

מסורה

ArtScroll Youth Series™

Rabbi Nosson Scherman / Rabbi Meir Zlotowitz

General Editors

The Story of
Rebbetzin Kanievsky

THE JAFFA EDITION

The Story of

by Naftali and Naomi Weinberger
with Nina Indig

Rebbetzin Kanievsky

A biography for young readers

Published by
Mesorah Publications, ltd

FIRST EDITION
First Impression … December 2012

Distributed in Europe by
LEHMANNS
Unit E, Viking Business Park
Rolling Mill Road
Jarow, Tyne & Wear, NE32 3DP
England

Distributed in Israel by
SIFRIATI / A. GITLER — BOOKS
6 Hayarkon Street
Bnei Brak 51127

Distributed in Australia and New Zealand
by **GOLDS WORLDS OF JUDAICA**
3-13 William Street
Balaclava, Melbourne 3183
Victoria, Australia

Distributed in South Africa by
KOLLEL BOOKSHOP
Northfield Centre,
17 Northfield Avenue
Glenhazel 2192, Johannesburg, South Africa

THE ARTSCROLL YOUTH SERIES™
THE STORY OF REBBETZIN KANIEVSKY
© Copyright 2012, by MESORAH PUBLICATIONS, Ltd.
4401 Second Avenue / Brooklyn, N.Y. 11232 / (718) 921-9000 / www.artscroll.com

---

ISBN 10: 1-4226-1333-X / ISBN 13: 978-1-4226-1333-7

Typography by CompuScribe at ArtScroll Studios, Ltd.

Printed in the United States of America
Bound by Sefercraft, Quality Bookbinders, Ltd., Brooklyn N.Y. 11232

This volume is lovingly dedicated to our children

Shani, Eli, Yakov, and Rikki

They had the great z'chus to visit
Rebbetzin Kanievsky ע״ה
and receive her berachah. That berachah is being fulfilled
every day, as they bring constant nachas to us
and to their grandparents.

The Rebbetzin was legendary for her kindness to children
and her concern for their well-being. We treasure our
moments with her and with **Maran Rav Chaim** שליט״א.
Their aura of kedushah, love for Klal Yisrael, and berachos
will always remain with us.

We pray that those warm memories will remain
with our dear children, young though they were,
and will inspire them to live up to the hopes of the Rav,
the Rebbetzin, our parents, and ourselves, as they grow
in Torah, yiras Shamayim, and service to our people.

Amir and Edna Jaffa

The inscription of Maran Harav Chaim Kanievsky *shlita* to the Jaffa family, who dedicated the biographies of the Rebbetzin

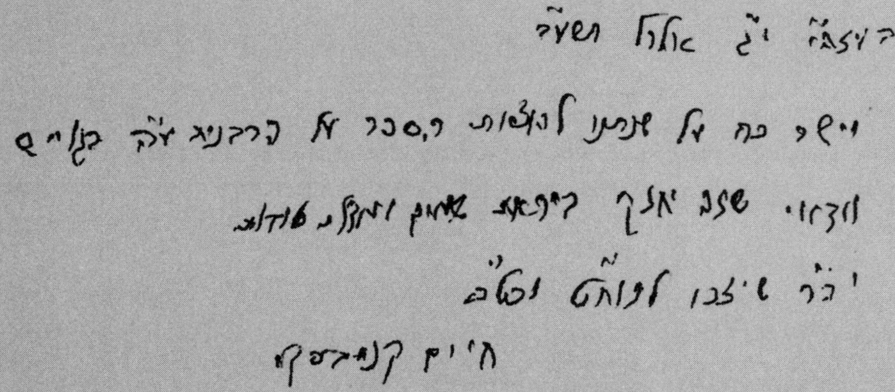
בעזה"י י"ג אלול תשע"ב

יישר כח על שתרמו להוצאת הספר על הרבנית ע"ה בלע"ז

ובודאי שזה יחזק יראת שמים ומדות טובות

יה"ר שיכתבו לחתימה טובה

חיים קניבסקי

בעזהש"י
13 Elul 5772

Y'yasher koach for contributing toward the publication of the book about the Rebbetzin ע"ה in English; this will certainly strengthen fear of Heaven and good *middos*.

May it be Hashem's Will that you be inscribed and sealed for a good year and all good, always.

Chaim Kanievsky

ב"ה ד' תמוז תשנ"ל

לכבוד ידידי הרב ר' נפתלי עפשטיין
שליט"א

שלום וברכה אחדשה"ט שמעתי שעומד ליתן ספר על דבר הרבנית ע"ה וראוי והגון הוא להגדיל תורה גודל ה' ית"ל זירא שמים ומעלות סובות כי הרבנית ע"ה היתה מיוחדת ומעלה וממצרת בכל מדות סובות הגונות עד למלא ובפרס במדת הסבלנות יה"ר שיהי' באמת לתועלת ותזכו לרוות רק נחת מכל יוצ"ח מתוך הרחבה

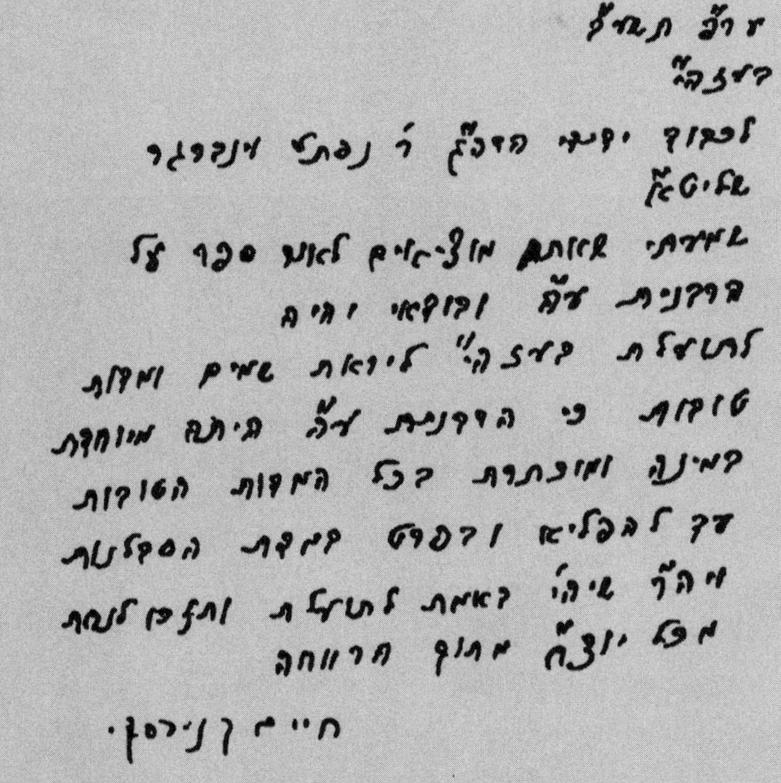

חיים קנייבסקי.

To my friend, Harav Hagaon R' Naftali Weinberger שליט"א,

I have heard that you are publishing a book about the Rebbetzin ה"ע.

It will surely be of benefit, with Hashem's help, to [inculcate] fear of Heaven and good character, because the Rebbetzin ה"ע was unique and was crowned with all good character traits to an amazing degree, and especially with the trait of patience.

May it be His will that it will truly be of benefit and may you merit nachas from all your offspring in comfort.

Chaim Kanievsky

Rabbi Meir Zlotowitz presenting the adult edition of the Rebbetzin's biography to
Maran Harav Chaim Kanievsky *shlita*

❧ Table of Contents

PHOTO CREDITS:

R' Moshe Barzam
Mrs. Yehudit Ben Abu
Ms. Chaya Braverman
R' Zelig and Brachah Braverman
Mrs. Miriam Cohen
R' Yaakov Cohen
R' David and Deena Epstein
R' Daniel and Fraidy Goldstein
R' Avraham Yeshayah and Chana
    Kanievsky
R' David Kanievsky
R' Shlomo and Tziporah Kanievsky

R' Yaakov Yisrael and Tova Kanievsky
R' Yitzchak Shaul and Sara Kanievsky
R' Yitzchak and Leah Koledetski
R' Shuki Lehrer
R' Yaakov Yisrael and Rivka Rochel
    Maklev
R' Avi Sarusi
R' Shraga and Chana Steinman
R' Yossi and Ruchie Stern
R' Yehoshua and Rutie Tzivyon
Ms. Tzipora Weinberger
R' Yaakov Yosef and Chana Winkler

A Visit with the Rebbetzin

Let's take a trip back in time. Not too far back, though. Pick a date between the 1970s and Succos of 2011. Now, imagine that you are going to visit Rebbetzin Batsheva Esther Kanievsky. You are very excited, but a little nervous, too. After all, she is such a great person, and you are simply…you. Will she be interested in your problem? Will she think it is silly or unimportant?

As you approach 23 Rechov Rashbam, you see two little old ladies sitting in front of the house. They are talking to each other and to the visitors going in and out of the Kanievskys' home. These ladies sit outside the house all day, almost every day, and they have been doing this for many years. The Rebbetzin does not mind that they sit there. She says, "I am always inspired by these two ladies because they are very careful not to speak *lashon hara*!"

Then you notice the long staircase leading up to the apartment. If it is a busy day, ladies and girls are waiting on the steps because there is no more room inside. There is a fan on the outside wall of the house to cool off the visitors on this hot day.

Finally you get into the house — but there are still many people ahead of you on line. If R' Chaim is learning somewhere else, the Rebbetzin tells the waiting people, "Go into the *cheder hasefarim* and sit in the Steipler's chair, or near it, and say *Tehillim*. May Hashem accept all your *tefillos*!"

And then it is your turn!

"I'm so sorry for keeping you waiting," the Rebbetzin says. "Would you like an Artik (ice pop)?" She gives one to you and takes one for herself, and you sit there and enjoy the cool treat together. Then she tells you some stories, usually about her grandchildren.

Hey! you might think, *I was so nervous about meeting the Rebbetzin, but this is just like visiting my grandmother!*

After a while you tell the Rebbetzin the reason for your visit. Maybe you are having problems in school, or maybe you did not get into the school you wanted. If you are a grown-up, maybe you are having problems at work or with *parnassah* or maybe someone is sick. No matter how old you are, no matter what you want to discuss, the Rebbetzin takes you seriously. She puts herself in your place and cries with you. She gives *berachos* and advice.

"The ways of Hashem are good," she says, "even though they are not always understood." By the time you leave, you are feeling much better about everything.

CHAPTER ONE
A Royal Family

Batsheva Elyashiv was born into a very important Torah family. Her mother's and her father's parents and grandparents were all *talmidei chachamim* or daughters of *talmidei chachamim*. You can almost say she was a "Torah princess"!

———— The Levins ————

Batsheva's grandfather (her mother's father), R' Aryeh Levin, was born in Poland in 1885 and moved to Eretz Yisrael when he was about 20 years old. A little while after he arrived, he married Tziporah Chana Shapira. They had a very simple wedding.

The Wedding Present

R' Aryeh was very poor. He was new in the country and still did not have a job. His parents lived far away and could not help out. He wanted to give his *kallah* a present after the *chuppah*, as other *chassanim* did. There was only one problem. He could not afford even a small gift.

R' Aryeh Levin

But then he had an idea.

"I would like to give you something in honor of our wedding," he told his new wife. "So this is what I will do: in the future, whenever we don't agree about something, I will always say that you are right."

Tziporah Chana thought that was a great idea. "And I will do the same for you!" she promised.

And that's exactly what happened!

In 1916, R' Aryeh became the principal of the Etz Chaim Talmud Torah, an elementary school in Yerushalayim. He was an excellent edu-

The Principal

cator who always made sure that his students had what they needed.

R' Aryeh noticed everything. If a boy was wearing torn shoes, he arranged for the child to get a new pair. If a boy was playing without a sweater or a coat, he found a way to provide one so his *talmid* would not freeze in the winter. And if a child looked hungry, he invited the boy into his office for breakfast.

What's more, he managed to do all this in a quiet way, offering it as a prize or giving an explanation so that the children or their families would not be embarrassed!

R' Levin had another job, too, as a prison chaplain (rabbi). In those days, Eretz Yisrael was ruled by the British. Many Jews wanted Eretz

The Visitor

Yisrael to be independent, and they fought against the British. Those who were caught were sent to jail, and that's where R' Aryeh went to visit them.

Every Shabbos morning after *Shacharis* he went to *daven Mussaf* with them and talk to them.

Rebbetzin Tziporah Chana sewed many pockets into her husband's clothes. In these pockets he would hide messages from the prisoners to their wives and families (there is an *eruv* in Yerushalayim, so he was allowed to carry). The British guards knew that R' Aryeh was bringing the letters, but they respected him and pretended not to notice. They

R' Aryeh Levin.
This photo hung in R' Elyashiv's apartment.

did not even ask to read the letters to make sure the prisoners were not telling secrets to their families or complaining about life in jail.

Because he took such good care of those in jail, R' Levin became known as the "father of the prisoners."

On Tuesdays and Fridays, R' Aryeh made other visits, he went to see patients in the hospital. He even went to people who had sicknesses that made others afraid to go visit them.

During Chol HaMoed Pesach and Succos, he took his grand-daughters, including Batsheva, to visit the widows of *talmidei chachamim*.

"They feel sad on Yom Tov," R' Levin explained to the girls. "That's when they remember the happier times when their husbands were still alive and they were not alone."

Batsheva went along with her grandfather on these visits for 12 years. When she grew up, she also visited *almanos* and the sick, and welcomed all types of people to her home. Growing up as a true "Torah princess" teaches a girl to understand the feelings of others, and to try to help them in many different ways.

One cold winter day, Rebbetzin Tziporah Chana Levin headed out to the grocery store.

A Cup and a Tub of Water

"I'm going out for a few minutes," she told her sons. "Please watch Shaina Chaya while I am away."

Right in front of her house, a poor man approached Tziporah Chana and asked for a drink. She had never seen this man before. "Would you mind waiting a few minutes while I go to the grocery store? But if you are very thirsty, I'll go upstairs and get you a drink right away."

He replied, "Please, I really need it now."

Tziporah Chana hurried back upstairs to get him a drink. While she was there, she checked on her children. The boys were very busy playing a game. But where was the baby, Shaina Chaya?

The frantic mother ran through the house. "Shaina Chaya, Shaina Chaya, where are you?"

She checked each room. Finally she found the little girl. While nobody was watching, she had fallen facedown into a tub full of water!

Tziporah Chana quickly plucked Shaina Chaya out of the water. She took care of the baby until she stopped choking and crying. Then she went to thank the poor man and bring him his drink — but the man had disappeared!

Rebbetzin Tziporah Chana's *chessed* had helped save her baby's life! Shaina Chaya grew up and became the mother of Rebbetzin Batsheva.

The Elyashivs

Batsheva's father, R' Yosef Shalom Elyashiv, *zt"l*, lived in Yerushalayim. He was a *posek hador*, a man who answered the hardest questions about Halachah. His grandfather was a famous *talmid chacham* who was known as the "Leshem," after the name of his *sefer*, *Leshem Shevo V'Achlamah*. His real name was R' Shlomo Elyashiv.

Happy with What They Had

R' Shlomo spent his days and nights learning. His wife, Batsheva Esther (after whom Batsheva was named), ran a grocery store. They did not own many things, but Batsheva Esther was satisfied with what they had. She did whatever she could so that her husband would be free to learn.

Her granddaughter was just like her. Not only did she have the same name, but she also was happy with very little, and her husband's learning was the most important thing in the world to her!

The Leshem and his wife had four children. Their daughter, Chaya Musha, married R' Avraham (Orener) Elyashiv, but they did not have children for many years.

The Miracle Baby

Chaya Musha used to *daven* and cry to Hashem, begging Him for a child. One day, she went down to the basement with her *sefer Tehillim* and began to weep bitterly. Her father, the Leshem, stopped by for a visit and heard his daughter crying. He went downstairs and wept and said *Tehillim* with her. Then he said, "My dear daughter Chaya Musha, I promise you that Hashem will give you a son who will light up the world with his Torah and *tzidkus*!"

Less than two years later, Chaya Musha's son was born. He was named Yosef Shalom, and he grew up to be a *posek hador*.

Rebbetzin Batsheva Kanievsky used to tell another story about what happened before her famous father was born.

Her grandmother Chaya Musha had a neighbor in Shavel, Lithuania, who had a bad temper. One day, Chaya Musha had just finished washing her laundry (by hand!) and hanging it on the clothesline to dry. Her neighbor passed by and cut the line. All the clean clothes fell onto the muddy ground and became dirty again.

Chaya Musha was upset, but she did not say anything. She quietly

R' Shlomo Elyashiv, "The Leshem"

Rav Avraham and Chaya Musha Elyashiv with their young son Yosef Shalom,
in Constantinople, Turkey, on their way to Eretz Yisroel.

picked up her laundry and washed everything again. As she washed and
rinsed and hung each item, she told herself over and over: *I must forgive my neighbor. I must not be angry. I must forgive my neighbor.* She
decided not to tell anyone what happened — not even her husband.

That evening, there was a knock on the door. It was the neighbor,
who came to apologize for her bad behavior earlier that day.

"After I got home," she said, sobbing, "my son suddenly got sick
with a high fever. I am so afraid that this is a punishment for what I did
to you. I really want my son to get better. Please, please forgive me!"

"Of course I forgive you," said Chaya Musha sincerely. "Go take
care of your child, and I will say *Tehillim* for his recovery."

The boy got better, and one year later Chaya Musha had her own
special baby boy!

A few years later, when Yosef Shalom was 12, the whole family
moved to Eretz Yisrael.

Young Yosef Shalom used to help his grandfather, the Leshem,
write his *sefarim*. The Leshem's eyes were very weak and he could

hardly see, so he spoke out loud and his grandson wrote down what he said. He also dictated letters to *gedolim*, and Yosef Shalom wrote the letters for him.

The Leshem passed away when Yosef Shalom was 16 years old.

R' Yosef Shalom Elyashiv

The Elyashiv-Levin Shidduch

Yosef Shalom Elyashiv married Shaina Chaya Levin in Yerushalayim in 1930. Both were about 20 years old.

From his wedding day until age 100, R' Elyashiv went to sleep between 10:30 and 11:00 every night and woke up at 3:00 in the morning, ready to start a new day. His wife, Shaina Chaya, rose with him and served him a cup of coffee at 3:30.

The Elyashiv Children

Rav and Rebbetzin Elyashiv had 12 children: five sons and seven daughters. Sadly, one son got very sick and died when he was 3 months old, and a baby girl was killed by a Jordanian mortar shell during Israel's War of Independence in 1948.

Batsheva Esther was the oldest girl. She was born in 1932, and was named after her father's grandmother, the Leshem's wife. The next child was named Sarah Rachel. It is interesting how she got her name.

The Elyashivs had a neighbor, an elderly widow named Sarah Rachel Goldman. Mrs. Goldman did not have children of her own. Rebbetzin Shaina Chaya Elyashiv, who was much younger than Mrs. Goldman, became her close friend.

One day, Mrs. Goldman said, "Shaina Chaya, when I pass on from this world, what will I leave behind? I have no children, so nobody will name a daughter after me. After a while, people will forget all about me."

Rebbetzin Shaina Chaya was so sad to hear Mrs. Goldman's words that she went home crying. She and her husband, R' Yosef Shalom, decided that if they would have a baby girl, they would name her in honor of their neighbor. This was unusual, because Ashkenazic Jews usually do not name children in honor of living people. But in this case, R' Elyashiv felt that making the old widow happy was more important than following this custom. "If someone does *chessed*," he explained, "they will not get hurt."

Mrs. Goldman was overjoyed! She was very grateful to the Elyashivs for the rest of her life. She had a special relationship with her little namesake and used to buy treats for her.

Rebbetzin Shaina Chaya did everything in her power to help her husband learn.

Outside the Dining Room

Once she served R' Yosef Shalom lunch at a small table near the front door of their house. Her father, R' Aryeh Levin, happened to stop by for a visit, and was surprised to see this. After R' Yosef Shalom went back to the *beis midrash*, R' Levin gently scolded his daughter. "Maybe you should respect your husband more and serve him in the dining room," he said. The dining room was also where some of the children slept at night.

Rebbetzin Shaina Chaya respectfully answered her father. "Abba," she said, "some of the children are sick in bed in the dining room. I did not want Yosef Shalom to see them, because then he would worry about the children. He would want to stay home and help me take care of them. I didn't want him to worry or to miss learning, so I served him his meal outside the dining room."

R' Elyashiv was very close to his daughters. Late on Shabbos afternoons he took walks with them. While they strolled, he told them

Shabbos Walks

Torah stories and answered their questions. Each girl had a chance to get her father's attention all to herself. These were very special times.

Once a month, their late Shabbos afternoon walk was to the Kosel HaMaaravi, where they davened. These visits to the Kosel ended in

1947, when groups of Arabs began to throw stones at Jews who were davening there and it became too dangerous to go.

The Elyashiv family did not have much money. They never went on vacation. The only time they ate poultry was on Shabbos, when they

Poor, but Rich all shared one small chicken. Meat was served only on Yom Tov. But the children were never hungry and they never felt deprived.

Even though they were poor, there was a little box in the kitchen into which the children put all their spare change during the year. The week before Pesach, Rebbetzin Shaina Chaya emptied the coins from the *kuppah* (box) and used the money to rent a room in a hotel. Then she sent her husband, R' Elyashiv, and one of their sons to the hotel. She did this because the house was noisy and busy before Pesach, and she wanted them to be able to learn in peace and quiet. One of their daughters brought them a hot meal every day.

The only time the Elyashiv children got new clothes was before Pesach. This was very common in their neighborhood. Shabbos HaGadol was the last time they had to wear their old and worn-out clothing, so the children called this day *"Shabbos HaShmattes"* (Shabbos of Rags).

Rebbetzin Shaina Chaya had only one *simchah* outfit. She wore it to the weddings of all her children and grandchildren. When her children offered to buy her a new dress, she answered with a smile, "The outfit I have is fine. Besides, I'm afraid that nobody will recognize me if I wear something different!"

In those days, most people did not have refrigerators. They used an icebox. Blocks of ice were placed inside to keep the food cold.

Cold Food, Warm Feelings When the ice melted, they had to have a new ice block delivered.

One day, Batsheva's brother, R' Avraham Elyashiv, won some money in the lottery and decided that he wanted to buy his parents a small refrigerator. His mother, Rebbetzin Chaya Shaina, said that he could only buy a refrigerator if he agreed to let the neighbors share it. She did not want to have any "luxuries" that the neighbors did not have.

Batsheva Elyashiv

The Student Batsheva was an excellent student at the Altshuler School and was well liked by others. Although she was shy, she got along with both the more and less popular girls. She had *simchas hachaim* and a friendly smile that made other people feel happy, too.

After class, she would patiently explain the day's lessons to the immigrants who had just come to Eretz Yisrael a little while ago and still did not understand Hebrew.

Many years later, she met an old classmate named Chana Leeder. "I'm not surprised that you are caring for so many people who come to you for advice," said Mrs. Leeder. "Even in school, you used to devote yourself to the other students!"

Batsheva Elyashiv in *gan* (kindergarten)

At home, Batsheva helped her mother care for the younger children. Even at night, if she heard one of her little brothers or sisters

The Big Sister crying, she jumped out of bed to get a pacifier and help the baby fall asleep. She did not want her parents to have to get up.

Batsheva's grandmother had the great idea that Batsheva should take a bookkeeping course. She took the course and graduated with

The Bookkeeper nearly perfect marks at age 15. Then she got a job. Every night, she fell asleep listening to the tune of her father's learning. When she awoke at 4:00 in the morning, she heard him learning again. She davened at sunrise, said *Tehillim*, ate some breakfast, and was at work by 8:00.

The first thing Batsheva did when she got paid was to figure out how much *maaser* money to give to *tzedakah*. Then she went to the grocery store and paid her family's bill. She gave the rest of the money to her parents. Even though the Elyashivs were poor, they were careful to give *maaser* from their earnings.

Batsheva saved only a little bit of her salary. She used that money to buy nosh for her sisters and brothers. Every Shabbos, she gave out treats for good behavior.

When the Leshem died, he left behind manuscripts of *sefarim* which were not printed during his lifetime. One of the manuscripts

The Transcriber was very hard to read. It was not yet ready to send to the printer. R' Yosef Shalom asked his teenaged daughter Batsheva to help out.

For about two years, she would return home from work and spend her evenings copying the entire volume. Her brother R' Moshe remembers his older sister sitting with their father as they worked together.

The *sefer* was then published by R' Elyashiv in 1948.

Someone in her family once asked Batsheva, "What did you do when you were young to earn the *zechus* of marrying R' Chaim Kanievsky, the great *talmid chacham*?"

Earning Her Reward

She answered, "Hashem is so good. He gives everyone what they want."

Her relative asked again, "But you must have done a special *chessed* that earned you this reward!"

Finally, Batsheva said, "During Israel's War of Independence, we moved in with my grandparents, the Levins, who lived in a safer part of Yerushalayim. There was not enough food for people to buy whatever they wanted. Every family got a ration card that they had to take with them to the distribution center to get food.

"I realized that my father was walking to the center in our old neighborhood and waiting on line. He was wasting time that he could have used for learning Torah! So I offered to walk to the distribution center and stand on line instead of him. That way, I brought the food home and my father was able to learn more.

"Maybe that is why I was rewarded with a husband who is so important in the Torah world!"

R' Chaim and the Rebbetzin visiting her father, R' Elyashiv

CHAPTER TWO
Another Royal Family

Batsheva felt very blessed to have R' Chaim Kanievsky for a husband. Just as she was a "Torah princess" who came from a family of Torah royalty, R' Chaim came from a royal Torah family as well.

The Kanievsky Family

R' Chaim's father was R' Yaakov Yisrael Kanievsky, who became known as the Steipler Gaon. He was born in 1899 in Hornosteipel, in the Ukraine.

R' Yaakov Yisrael Kanievsky: The Steipler Gaon

When Yaakov Yisrael was 11 years old, his father passed away. His mother, Rebbetzin Brachah, and her three young orphans were so poor that they had to eat their meals at other people's homes.

A few months after his father's death, Yaakov Yisrael was invited to go learn in the Novardok Yeshivah, which was far away. His mother agreed to let him go. "At least you will have what to eat there!" she said.

The Steipler as a young *maggid shuir*

He celebrated his *bar mitzvah* in the yeshivah. Not a single person from his family — not even his mother — was able to attend. During the regular Shabbos *seudah*, he delivered a *dvar Torah* that he had prepared himself. In honor of the occasion, Yaakov Yisrael received one special treat: fruit compote for dessert!

In later years, the Steipler hardly ever spoke about his childhood. He once told a family member, "My *bar mitzvah* was as simple as a *bar mitzvah* could be... however, I made good *kabbalos* (resolutions) on my *bar mitzvah* which have lasted throughout my life."

His relative was very curious to know what those *kabbalos* were. "What practices did you take upon yourself when you were only 13 years old?" he asked.

But the Steipler would not say.

When Yaakov Yisrael was only 18, he was sent to head a new branch of the Novardok yeshivah. Many people came to hear his *shiurim*.

The Karelitz Family

R' Chaim's mother, Rebbetzin Miriam Karelitz, came from a well-known Torah family. Her father was the Rav of Kossova. One of her

The Chazon Ish and His Sister

brothers was R' Avraham Yeshayah Karelitz, the famous *posek* who became known as the Chazon Ish. He was 20 years older than his little sister, but they remained close all their lives.

Many people believed that the Chazon Ish had *ruach hakodesh*, special help from Hashem to understand the Torah.

Ruach Hakodesh

His wife, Batya, ran a linen store and R' Avraham Yeshayah sometimes came at night to help with the paperwork. One night, he had a bad feeling. "I'm afraid the police are going to come check the store and make trouble for us tomorrow," he told Batya. The police in Russia were not friendly to Jews, and often hurt them in different ways. That night, the Chazon Ish and his wife moved all their merchandise from the store into the house.

When the police arrived the next day, they found nothing to inspect. They left the store without causing any problems!

Another time, while trying to escape from some soldiers, by mistake he went in the wrong direction. Instead of running away from them, he ran toward them. He passed between two rows of soldiers and they did not stop him. While he was running, he kept telling himself that he would be safe because he had just finished writing a *sefer*.

The Chazon Ish as a young man

The Chazon Ish went to visit R' Chaim Ozer Grodzenski, who was the leader of the yeshivah world at that time. He noticed a *sefer* called

The Kanievsky-Karelitz Shidduch

Shaarei Tevunah lying on the table. He picked it up and started to read it.

This sefer was written by a real talmid chacham, he thought.

The Chazon Ish found out that the author, R' Yaakov Yisrael Kanievsky, was still single. *Maybe he would be a good shidduch for my sister Miriam,* he thought.

R' Yaakov Yisrael Kanievsky married Miriam Karelitz. He took a position as a *maggid shiur* in the Novardok Yeshivah in Pinsk. The couple was very poor, but R' Yaakov Yisrael learned well and taught many *talmidim*.

Starting to build the Novardoker Yeshivah in Pinsk. The Steipler is at the far left (circled).

In 1928 their only son was born. They called him Shmaryahu Yosef Chaim, after both grandfathers. They also had two daughters, Yuspa and Ahuva.

R' Yaakov Yisrael only slept a little every night. Since he was awake anyway, he took care of baby Chaim. He tied a rope to the cradle. When Chaim cried in the middle of the night, R' Yaakov Yisrael tugged at the rope and rocked the baby back to sleep while singing *divrei Torah*.

Life in Bnei Brak

The Chazon Ish decided to move to Bnei Brak, in Eretz Yisrael. When he got there, he arranged for his sister Miriam and her husband, R' Yaakov Yisrael, and their children, Chaim, Yuspa, and Ahuva, to follow him. The Steipler's *talmidim* really did not want him to leave, but in 1934 the Kanievskys arrived in Eretz Yisrael. The trip, by boat, had

The Steipler with students of the yeshivah, when he was leaving Pinsk.
The Steipler is seated in the center, with the young Chaim Kanievsky standing in front of him.

lasted nearly three weeks. During that time, the Steipler and 6-year-old Chaim finished learning *Sefer Shemos* together.

The Kanievskys were very poor in Eretz Yisrael, too. On Shabbos, they usually had only challah to eat. On special Shabbosos they had a can of sardines with their challah. They almost never ate chicken or meat.

The Steipler became a *maggid shiur*.

One day, he asked his *talmidim* to come to his house to hear the *shiur*. When they arrived, he was in bed, covered with a blanket. After the *shiur*, the students asked him, "Rebbi, how are you feeling?"

"I am fine," responded the Steipler. "I am not sick. My only pair of pants is torn, and I'm waiting for my wife to come home and mend it. That's why I'm in bed!"

The Steipler became one of the leaders of the Torah world. He wrote many *sefarim*, including *Kehillas Yaakov* on the *Gemara*. These *sefarim* are still used throughout the world.

In 1947, the Chazon Ish, who did not have children, invited the Steipler and his family to share his apartment. He got permission from his landlord to subdivide the apartment. Now the Steipler and his son, Chaim, were able to spend more time learning with the Chazon Ish.

Talmidim of the Lomza Yeshiva and visting Rabbanim at a gathering at the home of
R' Reuven Katz, Rav of Petach Tikvah and Rosh Yeshivah of the Yeshivah.

After his *bar mitzvah*, Chaim went to learn in the Lomza Yeshivah in Petach Tikvah. He came home for Shabbos every week. After the *seudah*, he asked the Chazon Ish all the questions that had come up during the week. He even asked questions for other people who wanted answers from his famous uncle.

When Chaim got older and they began looking for a *shidduch*, it took about six years for him to get engaged. He used to say that none of the other suggested *shidduchim* worked out because when he started looking for his future wife, Batsheva Elyashiv was still too young to get married. He had to wait a few years for her to grow up!

CHAPTER THREE
R' Chaim and Rebbetzin Batsheva Kanievsky

--- **The Shidduch** ---

How did the *shidduch* come about between these two "royal" young people?

One day, R' Elyashiv (Batsheva's father) traveled to Bnei Brak to discuss some halachic questions with the Chazon Ish (R' Chaim's uncle). While they were talking, R' Elyashiv mentioned that he had older children. The Chazon Ish was very impressed with R' Elyashiv's understanding of Torah and Halachah, as well as his excellent *middos*. He suggested to his sister, Miriam, that if R' Elyashiv had a daughter who was ready to get married, she might be a good *shidduch* for R' Chaim!

R' Chaim Kanievky at age 20.

The Chazon Ish found out that Batsheva had the wonderful *middos* for which her Levin grandparents were famous. When he heard this, he worked hard to make the *shidduch* happen. He loved his nephew Chaim very much, and wanted the best wife for him!

R' Elyashiv visited R' Chaim in his yeshivah and talked to him in learning. And Rebbetzin Kanievsky visited Batsheva at work, and was very impressed with her. Finally, the two met a few times, and R' Chaim and Batsheva got engaged.

While she was a *kallah*, Batsheva was invited to spend Shabbos in Bnei Brak with her future in-laws and her *chassan*. She took a bus to

A Trip to Bnei Brak

Tel Aviv, and then a second bus to Bnei Brak.

When Batsheva showed up alone at the Kanievsky home in Bnei Brak, her future mother-in-law was surprised.

"Where's Chaim?" she asked.

Batsheva had no idea. She did not know that his parents had asked Chaim to meet her at the central bus station in Tel Aviv.

The Steipler figured it out. "Chaim is probably in the central bus station. He must have gotten so involved in his *Gemara* that he lost track of time and bus schedules. He's probably still there!"

The Steipler took a taxi to the bus station. Sure enough, there was R' Chaim on the bus platform, deep in learning!

The next time Batsheva was invited to Bnei Brak, she very politely told the Kanievskys not to go to the trouble of picking her up at the station. She would find her way to their house all by herself!

—————— A Simple Wedding ——————

R' Chaim Kanievsky married Batsheva Esther Elyashiv on Thursday, 7 Kislev 5712/December 6, 1951. It was the first wedding in the Elyashiv family, and was a very joyful occasion.

Batsheva Elyashiv's letter to her *chassan*:
"I ask that you not trouble yourselves to wait for me at the bus ..."

Shabbos *Sheva Berachos* took place in the house shared by the Kanievskys and the Chazon Ish. The only guest from Batsheva's family was her brother, Moshe, who learned nearby. Her father could not come, because he was a Rav and had to give a *shiur* in Yerushalayim. Fewer than 10 people were there for the simple Friday night meal. For the main course, everyone was served a chicken drumstick from the soup. Some *bachurim* came over at the end of the meal for *Sheva Berachos*.

Ten men were present for the Shabbos-day meal, and a few more for *seudah shelishis*. There was only one other *Sheva Berachos* meal, on Tuesday, also with very few guests.

בע"ה

קול ששון
קול חתן

עוד ישמע בערי יהודה ובחוצות ירושלים וקול שמחה
וקול כלה

ותחזינה עינינו בשובך לציון ברחמים לפ"ק

קול שמחה

חרינו מתכבדים בזה לחזמין את כב'
וב"ב לשמחת כלולת בננו היקר

הרב חיים שיחי'

עב"ג

הכלה המהוללה
מרת בת-שבע תחי'
בת הגאון ר' יוסף שלום שליט"א אלישוב
ירושלים

שתחי' אי"ה בסטומו"ץ ביום ה' מ' ויצא ז' כסלו תשי"ב
בשעה 3 אח"צ במתח-תקוה אולם .חצבי' רח' איכילוב.

בכבוד רב
יעקב ישראל קניבסקי ורעיתו

The invitation to
the wedding of
R' Chaim and
Batsheva Kanievsky

The actual invitation
Batsheva Elyashiv sent
her *chassan*.
The "handwriting" is
actually the impression
made on the invitation
when it was addressed
and postmarked.

בע"ה

נעלה את ירושלים על ראש שמחתנו

הננו מתכבדים להזמין את מע"כ ומשפחתו לכלולת בתנו

בת-שבע אסתר תחי'

עב"ג

החתן הרב חיים בהגרי"י שליט"א קניבסקי

שתחי' אי"ה בשעטו"מ ביום חמישי ויצא. ז' כסלו תשי"ב, בשעה 3 אהה"צ
באולם .הצבי' רחוב איכילוב מס' 11, פתח תקוה.

יוסף שלו' ושינא חי' אלישיב

The Chazon Ish at the wedding of R' Chaim and Batsheva Kanievsky

R' Chaim Kanievsky at his *chuppah*

At the wedding of R' Chaim and Batsheva Kanievsky.
(1) Rebbetzin Shaina Chaya Elyashiv (2) the *kallah*, Batsheva Kanievsky
(3) the *chassan*, R' Chaim Kanievsky (4) R' Yosef Shalom Elyashiv
(5) R' Reuven Katz (6) The Steipler

The Steipler and R' Chaim leaving from the house on Rechov HaRav Blau

Settling Down

R' Chaim and Batsheva lived in Petach Tikva, near the Lomza Yeshivah, until Pesach. R' Chaim's friend and *chavrusa*, R' Dov Weintraub,

Friends and Neighbors and his wife, Shulamit, lived nearby. Dov and Chaim knew each other since they were little boys in Europe. They played together as children, learned together in yeshivah, and continued learning together for many years.

After Pesach, the young Kanievskys moved to Bnei Brak. They shared a floor on Rechov HaRav Blau with three other couples, including their cousins the Karelitzes, the Weintraubs, and the Zakses. Each couple had one bedroom and a tiny kitchen. They all shared two bathrooms at the end of the hallway.

One year later, the Chazon Ish arranged for R' Chaim and Batsheva to move into a small two-bedroom apartment on Rechov

Babysitting children from the neighborhood

Ohr HaChaim. They shared the kitchen with the Schreibers. R' Pinchas Schreiber was very close to the Chazon Ish. Batsheva and Chaya Rosa Schreiber became very good friends. Chaya Rosa said that she never heard Batsheva raise her voice. People who knew them well said that in all the years Batsheva and Chaya Rosa shared a kitchen, they never had a single argument!

The Schreibers had a bit of a problem. Every day, Chaya Rosa returned from work an hour after her son Bunim came home from kin-

The Babysitter

dergarten. Who would watch Bunim until she got home? Batsheva said, "I get home from my bookkeeping job earlier than you. I am taking care of my children anyway. It's no trouble for me to watch Bunim along with my own children." For two years she babysat for Bunim Schreiber — for free!

Many years later, Bunim's son became engaged to Batsheva's grand-daughter. Batsheva was so happy! Was this her reward for watching Bunim so that R' Pinchas could learn in *kollel* for an extra 45 minutes every day? Batsheva was sure it was. Even though she had told Chaya Rosa that it was not hard to care for an additional child, 40 years later Batsheva admitted that it really had not been so easy.

Those years were very difficult ones in Eretz Yisrael. Sometimes all they had to eat was bread and potatoes. When he could, the Steipler

The Years of Poverty sent chicken or vegetables to R' Chaim and Batsheva. Batsheva served her husband these "fancy" foods, and she ate only bread with margarine.

"I want my husband to eat tasty meals so that he should be able to learn Torah," she said.

In 1959, R' Chaim and Batsheva moved to 23 Rechov Rashbam. This address on Rashbam Street later became famous all over the world as

23 Rechov Rashbam the place to go for *berachos* and advice from both R' Chaim and Rebbetzin Batsheva Kanievsky.

Building a Home:
———— The Kanievsky Children ————

R' Chaim and Batsheva had three boys and five girls. At first, there was no hospital in Bnei Brak, so the four older children were born in

Born in Yerushalayim Yerushalayim. In those days, it took about three hours to travel between the two cities. When it was close to the time for her children to be born, Batsheva (and her older children) moved into her parents' house to be closer to the hospital. Her mother also helped take care of her and the children after the new baby arrived.

R' Elyashiv with Rebbetzin Kanievsky

R' Chaim did not go to Yerushalayim with Batsheva before each baby was born. He stayed in Bnei Brak. He ate and slept in his parents' house and continued to learn in *kollel* until the babies were born.

The four younger Kanievsky children were born in Bnei Brak.

Once, Batsheva's father, R' Elyashiv, surprised her by coming to

Not Bitul Torah visit her and her newborn baby in the hospital. Batsheva was very happy to see him, but she had one concern.

"Abba," she said, "thank you for coming, but I'm worried about your *bitul Torah*." Batsheva did not want her father to "waste" time visiting her when he could have been learning Torah instead.

"Don't worry, Batsheva," said the *gadol*. "Visiting you is worth the *bitul Torah*!"

Chapter Three : R' Chaim and Rebbetzin Batsheva Kanievsky / 41

R' Gedaliah Nadel (r) with R' Chaim (c)

Batsheva wanted her children to grow up to be fine, *frum* Jews. From the time they were newborns, Batsheva washed their hands every

Starting Early single morning for *netilas yadayim*. The boys all wore yarmulkes from when they were under a year old. An elastic band kept the yarmulke from falling off their little heads.

The Lederman Shul is located a few steps away from 23 Rechov Rashbam. Its rabbi was R' Gedaliah Nadel, and he and his family lived

Their Other Children downstairs from the Kanievskys. Sadly, R' Gedaliah's wife, Rachel, passed away when her children were young.

Batsheva wanted to help the family, so she started cooking meals and sometimes even cleaning for the Nadels. When she prepared sandwiches for her own children to take to school, she sent sandwiches downstairs for the Nadel kids as well. She attended parent-teacher meetings at their school, and then went to tell R' Gedaliah what the teachers

Sender Preizler (l) accompanying R' Elazar Menachem Shach (r)

said. The younger Nadel children called Batsheva "Ima" because she treated them like her own.

Another child the Kanievskys took care of was Sender Preizler. He was a young orphan whose father died while serving in the Israeli Army. He started coming to the Kanievsky home to ask R' Chaim questions. R' Chaim finally said to him, "From now on, I will be your father and you will be my son." He invited Sender to the Friday-night *seudah*. That Shabbos, Rebbetzin Batsheva said, "Sender, just like R' Chaim is now your father, I will be your mother. From now on, please call me 'Ima.'"

For the next 29 years, Batsheva was like a mother to him in many ways. When Sender had a Shabbos off from yeshivah, he came to the Kanievskys. He slept in the hallway together with their sons, and ate his meals with the family. R' Chaim learned with Sender, and Batsheva spent a great deal of time talking to him about important matters. She even added an extra Shabbos candle for him every week.

R' Chaim and Batsheva were his *shadchanim* and helped him get married. They attended the *bris milah* of each of Sender's eight sons. Every Rosh Chodesh, when Batsheva sent her special stuffed peppers to her children, Sender and his family received a generous portion as well.

The Kanievskys helped him find a job as a sixth-grade *rebbi* in a good Talmud Torah in Bnei Brak. Today, R' Sender Preizler is a popular *rebbi* and storyteller. He is thankful to R' Chaim and Rebbetzin Batsheva for helping him succeed in life — with Hashem's help, of course!

R' Chaim and the Rebbetzin at the wedding of their oldest son, Avraham Yeshayah.
R' Dov Weintraub is in the background at left.

The Rebbetzin handled everything to do with the home. She did not ask R' Chaim or her sons for help with the chores. She sometimes allowed her girls to assist her, but usually she did every-thing herself, always with a smile.

The Best Mother

Batsheva kept the house neat and clean. She knew which foods each child liked, and remembered to serve them. She prepared freshly squeezed juices: different flavors for different children, according to what they liked.

The apartment was small — with only 2½ bedrooms — but the Kanievsky children grew up in a happy home and never felt as if they were missing anything. Even though Batsheva was very busy and many people came to visit her and ask for advice, she always had time for her children, and she never raised her voice.

"No matter how many people were there, my mother always said good-bye to me when I left the house to go learn in yeshivah," said R' Avraham Yeshayah when he was all grown up. "She sent me off with a package of food, *berachos* for success, and hugs and kisses."

The children learned good *middos* by watching how their parents behaved. The Rebbetzin often told the children how proud she was when they studied well or displayed good *middos*.

Even when something bad happened, Batsheva did not lose her temper.

Fire! In those days in Bnei Brak, kerosene heaters were used to warm the house in the winter. One day, Brachah was folding some clothing. By mistake, she put some clothes on the heater outside the kitchen, and they caught fire. R' Chaim made sure everyone was out and grabbed the notebooks in which he was writing his *sefer Derech Emunah* before leaving the house himself.

They stood outside, watching the firefighters put out the flames. R' Chaim turned to his wife with a smile. "*Baruch Hashem*, all our children are out safely, and I have my notebooks with me," he said.

"But what about the rest of the house?" asked the Rebbetzin.

"Don't worry," answered R' Chaim. "Because we have many *sefarim* in the house, everything will be fine."

After the flames were out and it was safe to go back into the house, they checked the damage. The kitchen and bathroom needed to be replaced. Some beds and chairs were burned to a crisp. But none of the *sefarim* was damaged!

What did her parents do to Brachah? Nothing. She was not scolded or blamed for the fire, and they all knew to be more careful.

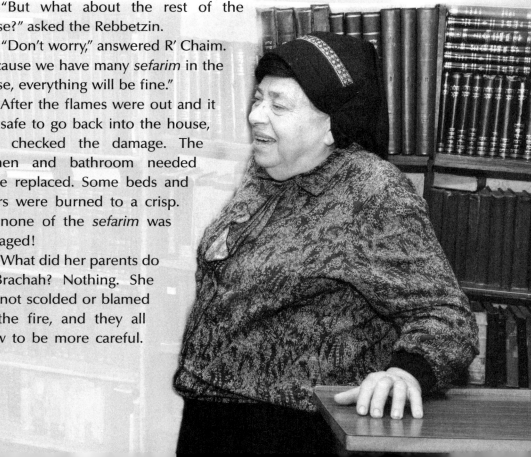

"Accidents happen," said the Rebbetzin. She knew that nothing occurs unless Hashem wants it to happen.

R' Chaim learned with his sons every day, helping them complete all or most of *Shas* even before they were *bar mitzvah*. All his sons still finish *Shas* every year.

The Best Father

Sometimes R' Chaim took Shabbos walks with his daughters. They discussed what happened during the week, and then he told them *Midrashim* and stories from the *Gemara*.

R' Chaim and his daughters also played "the *sefarim* game." There were many shelves of *sefarim* in the dining room, which they called the *cheder hasefarim* (*sefarim* room). R' Chaim asked his daughters to find a certain *sefer*, and then he read them a portion from the *sefer* and told them something interesting about the author.

One morning, the Rebbetzin woke up at her usual time — 2:30 — with a terrible sore throat. She felt ill and could not get out of bed. She usually prepared tea for R' Chaim at that hour. This morning, however, she felt too sick. She asked him to please prepare hot tea for both of them.

R' Chaim Tries to Help

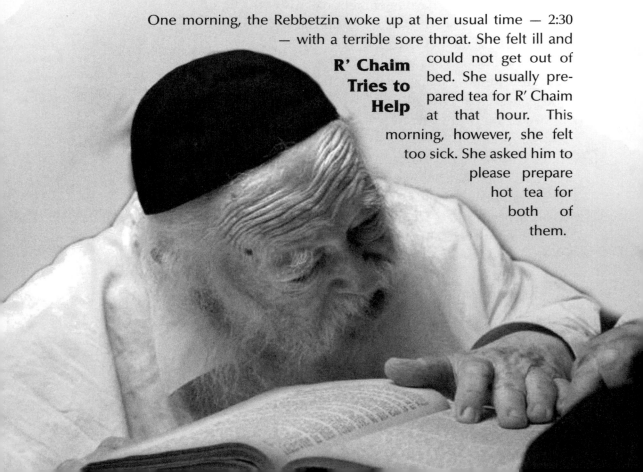

R' Chaim holding a *Sefer Torah* dedicated in memory of the Steipler

R' Chaim went to the kitchen, turned on the water, and put the kettle into the sink to fill. As the kettle filled up with water, he looked into his *sefer* and started to learn. Soon he was so busy learning that he forgot all about making the tea.

Almost half an hour went by and R' Chaim had not returned. Batsheva thought she heard the sound of running water. She managed to pull herself out of bed and into the kitchen. There was R' Chaim with his *sefer*, an overflowing kettle in the sink, and water all over the floor!

As Batsheva spent the next half-hour mopping up the water, she decided that she would never again ask R' Chaim for help in the house. It was more important for him to learn.

CHAPTER FOUR
A Wonderful Marriage

R' Chaim and Rebbetzin Batsheva had a very special marriage. The way they treated each other was a good example for others to follow. They respected each other and each appreciated what the other one did.

R' Chaim said he was able to learn better when Batsheva was home, and that he worried about her when she was away.

"I Learn Better When You Are Home"

One year, before Rosh Hashanah, Batsheva went to a neighbor's house to call her father. (The Kanievskys never owned a telephone!)

On the staircase to their apartment

"Abba," she said, "please forgive me for not coming to visit you before Rosh Hashanah. You know that my husband does not learn as well when I'm not home. I did not want to cause *bitul Torah*, so I could not come to visit you."

Of course, R' Elyashiv understood and agreed.

Batsheva stopped going to out-of-town weddings and other joy-ous occasions. She explained to people who invited her that if she was not home, R' Chaim did not learn as well. She did not want to be responsible for his *bitul Torah*. Most people understood.

When Henia Nadel got married in Bnei Brak, the Rebbetzin went to the *chuppah* and headed home as soon as it was over.

"Why are you leaving this wedding?" asked her neighbor, Reb-betzin Tzira Korlansky. "You are so close to the *kallah*! After her mother passed away, you helped raise Henia and her siblings. How can you leave so early?"

Batsheva responded, "I'm going home to prepare R' Chaim's sup-per. After he finishes eating, we'll walk back to the wedding together."

"Can't someone else serve R' Chaim his supper tonight?" asked Rebbetzin Korlansky.

"I don't let anyone else serve R' Chaim his lunch or supper. It's my greatest honor and I must do it every day! Besides, I don't want to cause any *bitul Torah*. R' Chaim told me that he cannot learn as well when I'm not home."

After the Rebbetzin served R' Chaim his supper, they walked back to the wedding, spent some time there, and then walked back home.

R' Chaim also treated the Rebbetzin with great respect. On Shab-bos, if she went to say *mazel tov* to a friend or neighbor who was

Waiting for His Wife
making a *simchah*, he waited to make *Kiddush*, often many hours, until she was home. He also insisted on personally making *Havdalah* for her. He waited patiently, *sefer* in hand, until she was ready.

R' Chaim and Rebbetzin Kanievsky woke up every morning at 2:30, way before it got light outside. Batsheva prepared tea and they spent

A Busy Schedule
a few minutes talking while they drank. Then R' Chaim said *Birchos HaTorah* and Batsheva answered *amen*. R' Chaim used the next two hours to learn. He had a very strict schedule, and worked hard every day to finish learning the

The *sefarim* for the Rebbetzin's *chovos* as she set them up each night, ready for the morning

amount he had set for himself. He called this learning his "*chovos,*" which means "debts" or "obligations." His *chovos* included *Tanach* and *Gemara, Rambam,* and *Shulchan Aruch.* Whatever pages he did not finish before *Shacharis,* he finished later in the morning.

For more than 35 years, the Rebbetzin had her own daily *seder* of *chovos,* as well. She learned her *chovos* early in the morning when they didn't interfere with her husband's learning. She started her *chovos* when her children were older and no longer needed a lot of attention.

A little before 3:00 a.m., she began her *chovos* by first saying *Birchos HaTorah.* She then learned from *Sefer Orchos Tzaddikim* and said the *Tehillim* for that day. Four *halachos* from the *Sefer Chofetz Chaim* followed, as well as the entire *Iggeres HaRamban, Perek Shirah,* and *Nishmas Kol Chai.* Her *seder* of *chovos* took about an hour and a half.

At 5:00 a.m., Batsheva answered *amen* to Rav Chaim's *Birchos HaShachar* (Morning Blessings), while the children were still sound asleep. Then R' Chaim put on his *tallis* and *tefillin* and walked to the Lederman Shul. When the children were older, Batsheva also went to

The Rebbetzin's seat in the Lederman Shul

shul. She said *Birchos HaShachar* there, so that others could answer *amen* to her *berachos* and she could answer *amen* to theirs.

After *davening Shacharis* at sunrise, they ate breakfast together.

Lunch was the main meal of the day. R' Chaim and Batsheva ate lunch with their children in the *cheder hasefarim* after *Minchah*. During lunch, R' Chaim would talk to the Rebbetzin and the children. Then he went to read and answer the many letters that came to him from all over the world.

Supper was a light meal that R' Chaim and Batsheva ate together in their small kitchen at about 8:00. They talked about their children and grandchildren. They also discussed important questions that people asked Batsheva. Other members of the family tried not to disturb them during these meals. The older children ate when R' Chaim and Batsheva were finished.

When the Kanievsky children were married and no longer took Shabbos-afternoon walks with their father, R' Chaim would go for a short walk with the Rebbetzin. They talked about the *chinuch* of their children and grandchildren, and about *emunah* and *bitachon*. R' Chaim sometimes reviewed Torah topics with his wife, especially those dealing with numbers, because Batsheva was very good in math.

R' Gedaliah Honigsberg, a grandson of the Kanievskys, has always spent a lot of time with his grandparents. He often heard his grandmother tell his grandfather, "Chaim, I love helping you with everything. I wish I could also help you with learning your *chovos*, writing your *sefarim*, and answering your letters. I'm not qualified to do that — but if I were able to, I would help you with all those things!"

Helping R' Chaim Learn

Batsheva did everything to make sure R' Chaim could devote himself to learning. She kept the house clean and took care of the children, cooked delicious meals and served them on time, and took care of all the family's money matters.

Until her third child was born, Batsheva worked as a bookkeeper in a food factory in Tel Aviv, and also part-time at a seminary in Bnei Brak. She became close to many of the students there. Girls would

come to her house in the evening to discuss personal matters, and Batsheva tried her best to advise them.

After Avraham Yeshayah was born, she stayed home to take care of the children. Sometimes she accepted small bookkeeping jobs that she could do at home. The extra money came in handy. In those early days, most of their income came from R' Chaim's *kollel* checks. Later on, they earned money by selling the *sefarim* that R' Chaim wrote.

R' Chaim never had to open the refrigerator to look for food, or even pour a drink. His Rebbetzin always knew what he needed and rushed to serve him. When he ate a meal without bread, she gently told him what *berachah* to say on each dish. She did not want him to waste time trying to figure out what ingredients went into each food on the plate.

Once she served him ice cream for dessert as a Rosh Chodesh treat. R' Chaim never ate ice cream before.

"Did you enjoy your dessert?" the Rebbetzin asked, as she took his bowl away.

"It was very tasty," answered R' Chaim, "but a little too cold for me."

In 2001, R' Chaim had a stroke. While he was recovering, Rebbetzin Batsheva stayed at his side for two weeks. The head of the hospital, Dr.

Always at His Side

Rothschild, provided a bed for the Rebbetzin so she could sleep there.

By that time, the Kanievsky children were all grown up. The Rebbetzin no longer needed to be home taking care of little children, so she was able to *daven* all three daily *tefillos* with a *minyan*. She did this every day at the Lederman Shul. Now, in the hospital, a small *minyan* was formed in R' Chaim's room. A *mechitzah* was provided so that the Rebbetzin could *daven* with the *minyan*.

By then, many people were coming every day to the Kanievsky home to get advice and *berachos* from the Rebbetzin. Some of them came to the hospital to see her. When R' Chaim was resting or learning with one of his sons, she hurried out to talk to the women who were waiting for her. Even though she strongly believed that she belonged

R' Elyashiv visiting R' Chaim in the hospital after R' Chaim had a stroke.

at her sick husband's side, she did not want to disappoint the women who came to her for help.

Batsheva believed that it was important to show R' Chaim that she was proud of him.

Coffee, Cake, and Compliments

One Friday morning, R' Chaim made a siyum during his regular learning seder. The Rebbetzin came in with cake and coffee for R' Chaim and his chavrusos as she did every week. But on this Friday, she served R' Chaim's coffee in an extra-large glass that she had never used before.

In front of their brother-in-law R' Yitzchak Zilberstein and the other men, the Rebbetzin said, "Chaim, there is a reason I brought in such a large glass. You deserve extra coffee today because you made a siyum. I'm so proud of you!"

R' Chaim learning with R' Yitzchok Zilberstein on a Friday morning

R' Chaim smiled and thanked her.

Later, the Rebbetzin explained to R' Tzvi Yabrov that it is very important to say nice things to other people. It's particularly important for a wife to praise her husband. Even though she usually praised R' Chaim in private, sometimes she wanted to compliment him in front of other people.

"The words a wife uses to praise her husband are the most important words she will say in her life," the Rebbetzin declared. "When people are married, they can never give each other too much praise."

CHAPTER FIVE
Batsheva, the Mother of Shikun Chazon Ish

The Rebbetzin lived at 23 Rechov Rashbam for more than 50 years. Her neighborhood was called "Shikun Chazon Ish" (the Chazon Ish neighborhood). The Lederman Shul was located just a few steps from the Kanievskys' home.

The Lederman Shul   23 Rashbam

Rebbetzin Batsheva Kanievsky was like a mother to all her neighbors. Women her age felt like her daughters. Teenagers and children

Simply Batsheva looked up to her. She cooked and baked, advised and taught, laughed and sang, and set an example in both *ruchniyus* and *gashmiyus*. She was everybody's best friend. The Rebbetzin visited new neighbors and helped out with their children. She knew most of the children by their first names. Most of the women and children called her simply "Batsheva" — not Rebbetzin.

Batsheva always had a wide smile on her face. As she walked to or from shul, she greeted everyone she met, grown-ups and children alike. Children loved the fact that she treated them as adults.

Batsheva loved doing favors for people.

She babysat for children who returned home from school before

Caring for the Children their mothers got home from work. She gave them drinks and snacks, but did not accept payment. She told everyone that she was happy to help out.

During the summer, Bnei Brak gets very hot and humid. Batsheva arranged trips to the ladies-only beach in Tel Aviv. About 10 or 20 girls went with her on the bus. The Rebbetzin brought along enough drinks and snacks for everyone.

On Shabbos afternoons, many children came to the Kanievskys' house for Shabbos treats. Batsheva always made sure to buy enough nosh for all the kids in the neighborhood, not only for her own family. On Rosh Chodesh she would make a "Rosh Chodesh party" for all the neighborhood girls. The guests enjoyed the treats, but even more, they enjoyed the Rebbetzin's compliments and attention.

Rabbi Yisrael Elya and Rebbetzin Ruth Weintraub lived next door to the Kanievskys for 49 years. The day after the Weintraubs moved in,

Celebrating Together

Batsheva knocked on their door and introduced herself. Then she started helping Rebbetzin Weintraub take care of her children.

One month later, the two ladies were chatting outside. They noticed that a *bris* was being celebrated in the Lederman Shul.

"I'm going over to say *mazel tov*!" Batsheva announced.

"Who is making a *bris*?" asked her new friend.

"I don't know, but I like to go to a *simchah* to say *mazel tov* — even if I don't know the people!" was Batsheva's cheerful answer.

Batsheva baked cakes and kugels for the *s'machos* of her friends and neighbors.

Before the bar mitzvah of one of the Weintraub boys, Batsheva

told his mother, "I will bake a cake for the *simchah*."

The day before the bar mitzvah, one of the Kanievsky children showed up at the Weintraubs' apartment carrying a large cake. A few minutes later, another one was delivered. And another. And another. And another.

Rebbetzin Weintraub ran upstairs to Batsheva. "Why did you bake five huge cakes?" she asked breathlessly. "This is much more than enough for the guests!"

Batsheva replied with a smile, "When I say one cake, I mean five cakes!" Then she hugged and kissed her friend and wished her *mazel tov*.

Helping the Sick

Batsheva knew a lot about medicine and doctors. People came to her for advice, and she often had suggestions about what to do to make someone feel better. She also knew the names of good doctors and hospitals, and when people asked, she told them where to go. Sometimes she went with women to the doctor or hospital, to make sure they were getting good care.

One of her neighbors had to go to a hospital in the United States. The Rebbetzin offered to watch her children until she and her husband came home from America. She cared for these children for two months in her own home!

She did the same for her nieces and nephews when her sister Shoshana Aliza Zilberstein had to be in the hospital. On Shabbos afternoons, the Kanievsky and Zilberstein children enjoyed playing together, and it got really noisy in the house. Batsheva took all the children to the tiny park in Bnei Brak. That way, R' Chaim could learn in peace and quiet and the children could have fun.

Batsheva thought of others while shopping, too.

Shopping

When she found out that one neighbor's son ate no fruits or vegetables besides avocados, she added avocados to her shopping list for him. When she heard that another neighbor's son was anemic, she sent him broiled liver — because that's what she gave her own child when he was anemic. It made no difference to Batsheva that these were not her own children. She treated everyone like her own family.

Someone who lived on a *moshav* in northern Eretz Yisrael wanted to sell fresh eggs in Bnei Brak. For close to 35 years, the Rebbetzin allowed him to sell the eggs from her steps on Rechov Rashbam. The *moshavnik* piled up the crates of eggs, and people paid the Rebbetzin.

The "Businesswoman"

Batsheva lost a lot of money while doing this *chessed*. Sometimes people forgot to pay, but the Rebbetzin always made sure the egg-seller received full payment — even if she had to take the money from her own pocket.

Once in a while, if there were leftover eggs, the seller allowed her to keep them.

Twice a week, other *moshavniks* would sell fresh produce outside the Lederman Shul. The Rebbetzin would ask her grandchildren to bring them cold drinks during the warm and humid Bnei Brak summer, and hot beverages during the winter.

No Vending Machines Needed

"Savta, I'm not in the mood to go downstairs now," a grandchild once complained. Then he added hopefully, "Maybe they brought their own drinks from the *moshav* today?"

The Rebbetzin replied, "Since I offer them drinks every week, they probably rely on me and don't bring their own refreshments. It is a *chessed* to do this. I will bring down the drinks myself."

At the end, the Rebbetzin and her grandson carried the drinks down together.

Rechov Rashbam used to be a dirt road. It was finally paved in the 1970s by a road-construction company that had both Jewish and Arab workers. Every day during the warm summer months, when the workers were pouring asphalt for the road, the Rebbetzin would go downstairs with a large container of cold drinks and real glasses from her kitchen.

"Please have a drink and give out the rest to your workers," she would tell the grateful foreman.

R' Chaim on Rechov Rashbam
before it was all paved

Very often, women asked the Rebbetzin for advice about how to get along with their neighbors.

Good Neighbors

"If you always look for ways to help your neighbors," she told them, "you will become good friends to each other."

The Rebbetzin was a perfect example of someone who followed her own advice. She gave everyone such attention, and showed each person so much love, that every woman believed she was the Rebbetzin's best friend!

Batsheva never wanted fancy things. Her wardrobe was simple, and so was her home.

Nothing Fancy

She never bought new clothes, only second-hand ones. Once in a while she allowed a rich lady in the neighborhood to buy her a Yom Tov outfit — only because this lady begged for the honor. But she only wore the new clothing on Yom Tov!

She refused to have anything "fancy" in the house. In later years, rich people wanted to give presents to her and R' Chaim. They thought these gifts would make the Kanievskys happy, or at least more comfortable. Batsheva always said no, thank you. She did not want to have anything that her neighbors did not have. She did not want anyone to come to their house, see something, and get jealous. She did not want anyone to go home and say, "I want to have a gold necklace or an air conditioner, or an elevator, or new linen — because the Kanievskys have it!"

Batsheva and R' Chaim received money from their parents, as a wedding present, to pay rent for two years. But their uncle, the Chazon **The Best** Ish, arranged for them to live rent-free in their apartment **Coat** on Rechov Ohr Hachaim. What should they do with the extra money?

First they asked their parents if it was all right to use the money for something else. When their parents gave permission, R' Chaim told his wife, "Batsheva, buy yourself a winter coat. You really need a new one. And buy some clothing for yourself and baby Chana."

Batsheva had a different idea. "You still don't own a set of *Shas*," she told her husband. "Buy yourself a set of *Gemaras* and some other *sefarim*. I can manage without a new coat."

R' Chaim finally agreed to buy *sefarim*. Many years later, Batsheva told her grandchildren that she had bought "the best coat ever!"

Batsheva was not interested in owning jewelry. She did not get an engagement ring when she became a *kallah* because her *chassan* and **Jewelry** his family could not afford one. After the wedding, her mother-in-law gave her a silver brooch. Batsheva later gave the pin to one of her daughters.

When she was much older, someone tried to get her to accept a gift of jewelry. A frequent guest to their home bought a gold necklace and gave it to R' Chaim. "Please give this to the Rebbetzin as a Yom Tov gift," the person said.

The Rebbetzin refused to even open the box.

"You deserve this for all the sacrifices you make for my learning!" said R' Chaim.

The Rebbetzin answered, "The gifts you give me that I enjoy are the *siyumim* that you make all year round, especially the *Siyum HaTorah* on Erev Pesach. Please give the necklace to somebody else."

When R' Chaim realized that Batsheva was not going to accept the necklace, he gave it to one of their daughters.

The Rebbetzin used to take care of her Braverman grandchildren so that her daughter Brachah could go to work.

New Three-Year-Old Boots Brachah wanted to thank her mother for helping out. She bought a pair of simple but warm winter boots and sent them to her mother as part of her *mishloach manos*. Even before the *Purim seudah* began, the Rebbetzin paid Brachah for the boots. She even gave Brachah more money than the boots cost! Then she stuffed the box into a closet.

About three years later, when the Rebbetzin's old boots were completely worn out, she began wearing the boots Brachah had bought for her. She used them for the rest of her life. Often during the winter, the Rebbetzin would thank her daughter for buying the boots.

"But Ima, you paid for them! They are yours!" Brachah would reply, and the Rebbetzin would say, "These boots make me feel so warm! Thank you so much for buying them!"

With Shlomo Braverman at his Bar Mitzvah

Chapter Five: Batsheva, the Mother of Shikun Chazon Ish / 63

The candlesticks, with lit candles, in the *cheder hasefarim*

A Simple Home

The Kanievsky home has no pictures or flowers, no breakfronts or elegant furniture. Their few pieces of silver are put away with the Pesach dishes and are used only once a year, at the Seder. Their single "fancy" possession is the silver menorah that R' Aryeh Levin gave his new grandson, R' Chaim, as a wedding present.

The dining room has a shaky table and a few plastic and folding chairs to sit on — not a matching set of furniture. High up on one wall is a shelf, lined in foil, that holds the Rebbetzin's collection of metal candlesticks that she lights before Shabbos.

But this room is the most important room in the house. It is called the *cheder hasefarim* because it has shelves and shelves of *sefarim* lining the walls. R' Chaim is very careful to put each *sefer* away exactly where it belongs. He does not want to waste time looking for a *sefer* that is out of place. He also does not like to see anything else put on the shelves besides *sefarim*.

There is a large wall unit with doors and drawers in the bedroom. This was a gift from Rebbetzin Miriam Kanievsky, R' Chaim's mother.

Batsheva assigned one drawer to each of her children. They were very happy to have someplace to put their personal things.

R' Chaim put a hammer, a few tools, and some clothing in his drawer. After his father, the Steipler, was *niftar*, one of R' Chaim's sons brought over the Steipler's clothing. R' Chaim never wore his father's clothes. They were put into a top drawer of the wall unit.

Batsheva's clothes were kept in a bottom drawer. When she was older, her assistant, Mrs. Miriam Cohen, noticed that it was hard for her to bend down to get her things. "Please move the Steipler's clothes to the bottom drawer, and use the top one for yourself," she begged. But Batsheva refused. "These clothes belonged to a *tzaddik*, so they belong on the top," she said. "Besides, it really doesn't bother me to bend down."

Three years before the Rebbetzin's *petirah*, one of her other helpers put Batsheva's things into the top drawer. "I know you didn't want to switch drawers," she told the Rebbetzin, "but it hurts me to see you bending down."

The Rebbetzin did not want to "hurt" her helper, so she agreed to leave everything where it was.

The Kanievskys' wall unit

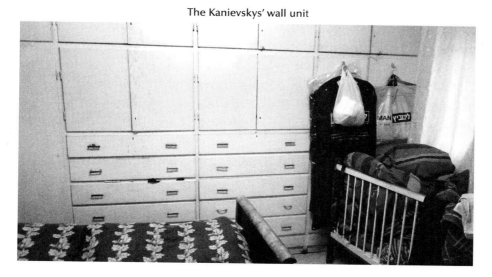

Modern Conveniences

The Rebbetzin's children chipped in and bought their mother a blender.

The Blender "Thank you," she said, "but I really do not need this. Hashem gave me two healthy hands to work with. I don't need this luxury item."

"But Ima," pleaded her children, "if you use a blender, food preparation will go so much faster! You'll be able to prepare much more food in the same amount of time. Imagine how many more guests you'll be able to invite!"

This was the only argument that could have convinced the Rebbetzin to accept their gift — so she did.

For many months a year, Bnei Brak is hot and humid. Yet for a very long time, the Kanievskys did not own an air conditioner. When sup-

Air-Conditioning porters offered to buy them a unit, they refused.

"No, thank you," they replied. "We have managed without air-conditioning until now, and *im yirtzeh Hashem* we will continue to manage without air-conditioning in the future. We do not want to have something that many of our neighbors do not have."

After many years, some people convinced them that an air conditioner might be better for R' Chaim's learning, so they agreed to try using an air conditioner. If it would help R' Chaim learn, they would consider buying one.

Indeed, R' Chaim found it easier to learn when the air was cooler and less humid. So they installed the unit in the *cheder hasefarim*.

Rebbetzin Batsheva was not comfortable having such a "luxury" in the house. She spent most of her time in the part of the house without air-conditioning, and hardly went into the *cheder hasefarim*. When R' Chaim was not home, she turned the unit off.

People then begged her for the honor of putting an air conditioner in her kitchen. The Rebbetzin spent much time in that tiny space, cooking for her family, neighbors, and the needy.

"No," she insisted. "I don't want anyone to say, 'Rebbetzin Kanievsky's kitchen is air-conditioned. I want air-conditioning in my kitchen, too.'"

For the last two months of her life, she finally had an air-conditioned kitchen. How did this happen?

R' Yitzchak Ohev-Tzion, a *rosh kollel*, told the Rebbetzin that her helper Mrs. Cohen was very uncomfortable in the hot kitchen.

"Why didn't she tell me this before?" asked the Rebbetzin.

"Because she knows how important it is for you not to have luxuries in your home," the *rosh kollel* replied.

"If Miriam is uncomfortable," said the Rebbetzin, "I'm willing to buy one."

When the air conditioner arrived two days later, the Rebbetzin hugged and kissed Mrs. Cohen. "I agreed to get this air conditioner just for you!" she said. "I am so sorry if I made you feel hot and uncomfortable!"

The New Oven

The Rebbetzin had an old oven that was always breaking. First one part broke, and when it was fixed, another one soon needed to be replaced. The repair company had a hard time finding parts to fit the old oven. "It's time to buy a new oven," the repairman finally said.

The Rebbetzin refused.

The Rebbetzin's oven

Finally, her children decided to act. They ordered a new oven for their mother. One night, when the Rebbetzin was at a local *simchah*, they had it delivered and installed. The old oven was taken away.

When the Rebbetzin came home and saw the new oven, she burst into tears. "I don't need this fancy new oven!" she cried. "Besides, I miss my old oven. I used it so many times for the *mitzvah* of *hafrashas challah*!"

Her family was sad to see how much pain their kind act caused their mother. The next day, they had the new oven taken back, and the old oven was returned and installed again in the Rebbetzin's kitchen. This oven stayed in her home until three years before her *petirah*, when it could no longer be repaired.

No Phone Reception

Rebbetzin Batsheva and R' Chaim never owned a telephone. They did not have a landline or a cell phone. They were afraid that if they had a phone, it would never stop ringing. People would call all day and all night, and disturb R' Chaim's learning.

When she needed to make a call, the Rebbetzin simply borrowed someone else's phone.

Making the Beds

Brachah Kanievsky married R' Zelig Braverman in the 1980s. It bothered the young couple that they had comfortable new mattresses while R' Chaim and the Rebbetzin slept on old ones. They decided to buy their parents a new set.

When the new mattresses were delivered, the Rebbetzin first ran over to Brachah's house and paid her for them. Then she sent the mattresses to another family!

"They need them more than we do," she explained to her daughter and son-in-law.

Years later, her children bought a new set of linen for their parents. They removed the sheets and pillow cases from the package and made the beds. *If we give them a wrapped package, Ima will send it back to the store. If we put the sheets on the beds, she won't be able to return them!* they thought.

Of course, when the Rebbetzin saw the new sheets on the beds, she begged her children to take them back, but they refused. So the Rebbetzin and R' Chaim used the set for a little while.

With her son-in-law R' Zelig Braverman

One day, someone noticed that the linen had not been on the beds for a while. "Ima, what happened to the linen we bought you?"

The Rebbetzin explained. "You know that both Abba and I usually sleep for only three hours. We really don't need new linen. We hardly use our beds. But our neighbor 'Mrs. Adler' told me that she wasn't feeling well and the doctor told her to get at least eight hours of sleep every night. I thought we would get better use of the linen by giving the set to Mrs. Adler!"

A poor person who lived in Bnei Brak needed to find money to pay for his daughter's wedding. He came to the Rebbetzin to discuss

The Kiddush Cup
"a very good idea" that he had.

"I have a rich cousin in America who admires R' Chaim and learns from his *sefarim*," he said. "My cousin would love to own something special that belonged to R' Chaim. If you would give me R' Chaim's silver *Kiddush* cup — the one he has been using on Shabbos and Yom Tov for more than 25 years — I could sell it to my American relative for a lot of money. I could probably get enough money to pay for my daughter's wedding!"

"Of course!" the Rebbetzin agreed, and she gave the man R' Chaim's *Kiddush* cup right away.

A few hours later, the man returned with a *Kiddush* cup in his hand. "Here is another *becher* for R' Chaim to use," he said. He had returned a silver-plated cup in exchange for R' Chaim's silver one.

One of the Rebbetzin's granddaughters asked the Rebbetzin, "How could you allow that person to give back a silver-plated *Kiddush* cup? The one you gave him was pure silver! Besides, it was valuable, because his cousin will pay a lot of money for Sabba's *Kiddush* cup!"

The Rebbetzin replied, "Do you think Sabba cares whether it's real silver or not? Obviously, this man is poor and cannot afford to buy real silver. Now I'm even happier that I gave him Sabba's cup! We did a big *mitzvah* by helping him pay for his daughter's wedding!"

R' Chaim used this silver-plated *becher* for several years.

On Chol Hamoed Pesach and Succos, R' Chaim and the Rebbetzin would visit their newly married grandchildren.

A Valuable Lesson

One grandchild remembers a particular visit. "Right after we got married, we had a cabinet with silver miniatures in the dining room, but we still did not have a bookcase for *sefarim*. This bothered Sabba. As he was leaving, he pulled me to the side and, with a twinkle in his eye, he said, "I give you a *berachah* that you should be *zocheh* to remove the '*shmattes*' (rags, junk) and replace them with *sefarim*!"

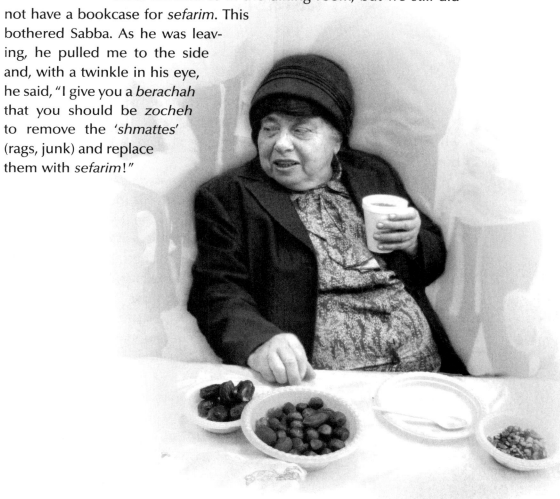

CHAPTER SIX
Hafrashas Challah

One of the mitzvos that is especially for women (although men do it, too) is *hafrashas challah*, separating "challah," a small piece of dough, when baking. In our times, the piece of challah that is separated is burnt.

When Batsheva was a young girl, *hafrashas challah* was a highlight of the week in the Elyashiv home. Rebbetzin Shaina Chaya and her daughters did this *mitzvah* every single Thursday night. They prepared the dough, made the *berachah,* and pulled off a portion to burn as *"challah."* Then they said the special *Yehi Ratzon* and *Tehillim.*

Starting Young

Rebbetzin Shaina Chaya Elyashiv with her daughter, Rebbetzin Batsheva Kanievsky

The Elyashivs did not have an oven. The two older girls, Batsheva and Sarah, carried the braided dough in large metal pans to a bakery. The walk took five minutes each way, and the pans were heavy. For a few *grushim* ("pennies"), they were allowed to bake the challos in the bakery's oven. When the challos were baked and the pans had cooled down, Batsheva and Sarah brought the challos home.

The Rebbetzin with her son R' Shlomo and grandchildren

After her marriage, Rebbetzin Kanievsky performed *hafrashas challah* most Friday mornings. But sometimes she bought bakery challos for Shabbos.

Commitment

In 1967, two accidents happened to members of the Kanievsky family. R' Chaim fell into a hole in the ground on his way to *kollel* and needed to spend eight months in bed to recover. A little while later, their son R' Shlomo was hit by a car and spent a long time in the hospital.

The Rebbetzin thanked Hashem for healing her husband and for sparing their son's life. To show her gratitude, she decided to take on the *mitzvah* of separating *challah* every week.

Making challah was hard work. There were no electric mixers, and the dough had to be kneaded by hand. The entire process took several hours.

The First Oven

The Rebbetzin prepared the dough at home, separated *challah*, braided the challos, and placed them in pans. At that time, the Kanievskys did not yet own an oven. She stacked the heavy pans of challos on top of each other. Then she lugged them to the Vizhnitz bakery, 10 minutes from her house.

Sometimes one or more of her children went along to help. Usually it was Avraham Yeshayah, the strongest. Sometimes he waited in the bakery until the challos were baked. Other times, he came back later in the evening to pick up the freshly baked loaves.

With *challos* baked for a *Hachnasas Sefer Torah* at R' Shlomo Kanievsky's Yeshivas Kiryat Melech

R' Chaim saw how hard it was for his wife to bake challos. He asked his children if he could do anything to make it easier for her.

"Maybe you should buy an oven so that the *hafrashas challah* and baking could take place at home," they said. "That way, Ima won't have to trudge to the bakery with the heavy pans, wait, and then carry the challos home." R' Chaim gladly agreed, and gave them money to buy an oven and have it installed.

Later that week, workers arrived to install the new oven. At first the Rebbetzin refused. "This is not necessary!" she said.

"But, Ima, this is a gift from Abba to make it easier to do the *mitzvah*!" they explained.

Only then did she agree to have the oven put in.

Over the years, many women all over the world learned how to do *hafrashas challah* by watching Rebbetzin Kanievsky separate *challah* in her kitchen. Many women then started to do this *mitzvah* themselves, every week.

It was the first Erev Shabbos after the Rebbetzin decided to do *hafrashas challah* every week. She was so excited to do the *mitzvah* that she baked many more challos than she needed. That same week, there was a problem with a machine at the Vizhnitz bakery. There were not enough challos in Bnei Brak for Shabbos!

A Sign from Above

The Rebbetzin sent challos to her father-in-law, the Steipler, and to some other *rabbanim* and *roshei yeshivah*. If not for her extra baking, they might not have had challos for Shabbos at all!

The Rebbetzin took this as a sign from Hashem that she should continue doing *hafrashas challah* every single week. From then on, there wasn't one week that she missed baking challah, and she also continued to send challos to other people for Shabbos.

Beginning in 1967, the Rebbetzin did *hafrashas challah* every Friday morning. In later years, she changed the time to Thursday afternoon.

The Rebbetzin's Hafrashas Challah

This way, she could teach women how to do the *mitzvah* while not interfering with the Friday-morning preparations for Shabbos.

Before separating the *challah*, the Rebbetzin explained the *halachos* to the women and girls who gathered around her. Afterward, when the women told her how wonderful the *mitzvah* was, she asked them to try to separate *challah* themselves in their own homes.

The Rebbetzin made the *berachah* of *hafrashas challah* and then *davened* and talked to Hashem for about 10 minutes. She offered *tefillos* straight from her heart for all the problems she always heard about.

Separating *challah*

Then she said the special *Yehi Ratzon* after the *hafrashas challah*. Afterward, she went through all the requests from the women who came, and gave them *berachos*.

As the years went by, more and more women came to watch the Rebbetzin's *hafrashas challah*, until she had about 150 women weekly. Only about 15 women were able to join her in the tiny kitchen. (The kitchen was even too small for their refrigerator to fit in! They kept it in the bedroom.) Most women gathered in the *cheder hasefarim*. The Rebbetzin made a loud *berachah* and the women responded with a thundering *Amen*.

Every Day

The Rebbetzin loved this *mitzvah* very much. For more than 20 years, rain or shine, on every weekday morning that she did not bake challos at home, she went to the Vizhnitz bakery to do *hafrashas challah*.

Sometimes she walked over in the early-morning hours, before dawn. Sometimes she first served R' Chaim his breakfast and went to the bakery afterward.

In the bakery, the Rebbetzin made the *berachah*, separated *challah*, and *davened* for the people who came to her and R' Chaim for *berachos*. On days that she separated *challah* in her home, she usually didn't go to the bakery.

If the Rebbetzin did not feel well, or it was not "walking weather," she still did not miss a day of *hafrashas challah*. Even when she broke her shoulder and was in great pain, she insisted on doing her special *mitzvah*.

The Recipe for Success

For more than 15 years, after the Rebbetzin completed *hafrashas challah* at home and the dough was ready to be braided, the Rebbetzin would ask her neighbor Mrs. Lederman to braid the challos. Mrs. Lederman was an older woman who had no children, and she was very honored by this request. She always made sure to do all her Shabbos shopping early so that she would be ready in time to braid the challos.

When Mrs. Lederman got very old and could no longer come to the Rebbetzin's home, the Rebbetzin would send her daughters with pans of dough to Mrs. Lederman. "Please tell Mrs. Lederman that I need her expert challah-braiding skills to help the challos come out beautiful and delicious," she instructed.

"Mrs. Lederman appreciates being asked to braid the challos," the Rebbetzin told her daughter Brachah on several occasions. "It means so much to her that her skills are needed. This is probably why the challos taste so delicious whenever she braids them!"

Sometimes the Rebbetzin told women to do the *mitzvah* of *hafrashas challah* in order to have healthy babies or a *refuah sheleimah*.

In the Zechus of Hafrashas Challah

Mrs. C.R.E., a young mother who lived in the Kanievskys' neighborhood, was very sick in the hospital. Her family rushed to the Rebbetzin and asked for a *berachah*. The Rebbetzin advised that all the women of Mrs. C.R.E.'s family should do *hafrashas challah*.

"Would you visit her?" they asked.

"Of course!" the Rebbetzin responded.

She went to the hospital and gave Mrs. C.R.E. many *berachos* in the emergency room. Then the Rebbetzin said, "Please accept upon yourself to complete the *mitzvah* of *hafrashas challah* every Thursday night or Friday afternoon, and Hashem will give you a *refuah sheleimah*."

Mrs. C.R.E. was very weak and sleepy, but she nodded her head in agreement. Her mother hurried home and prepared a batch

The Rebbetzin *davening* after *hafrashas challah.*

of dough. She returned to the emergency room with the large bowl of dough, and Mrs. C.R.E. separated *challah* with a *berachah.*

The Rebbetzin heard that the patient had separated *challah* in the emergency room. She said, "Such *mesirus nefesh* for such a special *mitzvah*! I'm sure she will get better soon." And she did.

Since then, Mrs. C.R.E. has performed *hafrashas challah* with a *berachah* every single Erev Shabbos and Erev Yom Tov!

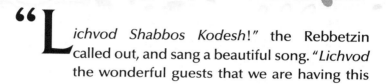

CHAPTER SEVEN
Shabbos

"**L**ichvod Shabbos Kodesh!" the Rebbetzin called out, and sang a beautiful song. "*Lichvod* the wonderful guests that we are having this Shabbos!"

Rebbetzin Kanievsky was in her little kitchen, cooking and baking for Shabbos. Even as a young mother with no extra money, she man-

Singing in the Kitchen aged to send her neighbors small food packages to show how much she cared for them. When R' Chaim

became well known and people were buying his *sefarim*, the Kanievskys were able to afford more. Every Erev Shabbos the Rebbetzin and her assistants would prepare food for family, friends, neighbors, guests, and needy people. In her later years, they sent fish, kugels, salads, challah, and cake to nearly 100 families every week!

"Who is on your food list?" her grandchildren would ask.

The Rebbetzin would never give a straight answer to this question. "I wish I could send food to every Jewish family in the world," she would exclaim, "and make everyone happy in honor of Shabbos!"

If she was baking a cake or a kugel for an *aufruf* or *sheva berachos*, she piled blessings on the *chassan* and *kallah*. "Hashem, please make sure that they have a happy marriage, many healthy children, and a lot of *nachas*!" And she sang some more. If she was preparing food for a *kiddush* or a *bris*, she sang out her *berachos* for the parents and the new baby.

Her granddaughters, who helped her in the kitchen, learned many beautiful *niggunim* and songs from the Rebbetzin, and would sometimes sing along with her.

She always decorated her cakes with colorful sprinkles so that even young children would enjoy her delicious and appetizing goodies.

"Mrs. Z." was a widow who lived not far from the Kanievskys. Before every Shabbos and Yom Tov, the Rebbetzin would send her a

Chocolate Cake for an Almanah

delicious home-baked chocolate cake from her kitchen. Some weeks the Rebbetzin would add a handwritten note filled with *berachos* and good wishes. Although she was always busy, the Rebbetzin never forgot to send the *almanah* her chocolate cake. One of her granddaughters would deliver it each week.

In the kitchen, with a grandson

After the Rebbetzin's *petirah*, Mrs. Z. came to comfort the mourners. "When my husband passed away, it was the saddest time of my life," she told the Rebbetzin's daughters, with tears streaming from her eyes. "What gave me the most comfort was the chocolate cake your Ima sent me every week.

"Of course, the cake was always tasty. But what I appreciated much more than the cake was that your mother thought about me every week and felt my pain. This made me realize that there were people who still cared about me and loved me. Your mother's thoughtfulness always made me feel better."

Mrs. Z. would have been amazed to know that she was only one of the many people whose lives the Rebbetzin touched every week.

Mrs. Rutie Goodman lived near the Rebbetzin. Her mother died when she was a teenager, and the Rebbetzin treated her like a daugh-

Fish for the Goodmans

ter. When she was married, the Rebbetzin visited her in the hospital every time she had a baby. She brought Rutie packages of home-cooked foods, and invited her husband and children for Shabbos meals.

After Rutie's fourth child was born, the Rebbetzin started sending fish every Erev Shabbos and Erev Yom Tov to the Goodman family.

"It's really not necessary!" Mrs. Goodman protested. She did not want the Rebbetzin to spend time cooking for her.

"Don't worry, I'll only send it for a short time," the Rebbetzin assured her.

The Rebbetzin's "short time" turned into 18½ years of sending gefilte fish to the Goodmans every Erev Shabbos and Erev Yom Tov. After each baby was born, the Rebbetzin added another half

The Rebbetzin's fish pot

roll. She also sent taffies and candies for the children. For Shabbos Chanukah she added jelly doughnuts as a special treat.

When the Rebbetzin broke her shoulder, Mrs. Goodman offered to help out. "Thank you," said the Rebbetzin. "I am fine and don't need any help. But don't worry — I'll send you fish for Shabbos as usual!" Nothing Rutie said could change the Rebbetzin's mind.

When the Goodmans were expecting guests for Shabbos, Rutie didn't know what to do. If she told the Rebbetzin about her company, the Rebbetzin would send more fish. But Rutie didn't want her to cook even more than usual! If Rutie didn't tell her and the Rebbetzin found out, she would ask, "Why didn't you tell me you were having guests? I would have sent more fish!"

The year of the Rebbetzin's *petirah*, the first day of Succos was a Thursday. Of course, the Rebbetzin sent fish on Wednesday morning for Yom Tov. When Mrs. Goodman met the Rebbetzin on Yom Tov, she thanked her.

"Please do not send more fish tomorrow," she said. "We have enough for Shabbos."

The kitchen

"I'm cooking anyway tomorrow," said the Rebbetzin. So she sent fish to Mrs. Goodman on Friday as well.

The Rebbetzin passed away the next day, on Shabbos Chol HaMoed.

That Shabbos was one of the most difficult Shabbosos of Mrs. Goodman's life. As she and her family ate the Rebbetzin's delicious fish during *seudah shelishis*, they tried hard not to cry. They already knew the sad news; however, on Shabbos it is forbidden to mourn. But they were all thinking about the years of fish and packages that the Rebbetzin sent, along with lots and lots of love.

Eggplant Salad

The Talmud teaches that every year, on Rosh Hashanah, Hashem decides how much money each person will have for the year. A few things are not included in this sum, such as how much money a person spends on food for Shabbos. If a person spends more for Shabbos food, he receives more money.

One of the foods the Rebbetzin sent people every Shabbos was her special, deep-fried eggplant. One year, eggplants were very expensive.

Her assistant Miriam Cohen suggested, "Perhaps we should not buy eggplants for a few weeks, until the price comes down? We can make other foods. I'm sure everyone will enjoy them."

"Of course we can send new foods also," said the Rebbetzin. "But everyone is used to getting eggplant for Shabbos.

"We must not worry about the price. Hashem pays us back for what we spend on Shabbos food!"

Erev Shabbos Minchah

By the time the Rebbetzin's children were all grown up, she used to *daven* three times a day with a *minyan* at the Lederman Shul next door. The only time she didn't do this was for *Minchah* on Friday afternoon. Then she was busy in the kitchen preparing for Shabbos, so she *davened* at home.

Exactly on time, she took off her red-and-white Erev Shabbos apron. She put on her Shabbos shoes, washed her hands, and got ready for *Minchah*. Ten minutes later, the Rebbetzin was in the hallway of her home overlooking the shul, *davening* with the *minyan*. After *davening*, she continued her Shabbos preparations.

The Rebbetzin felt bad about not being able to go to shul on Friday afternoon. But wearing her Shabbos shoes on a weekday made her feel like she was giving more honor to the *tefillah* — even though she was *davening* at home.

Hadlakas neiros before Shabbos was a very special time for the Rebbetzin. All who watched her light candles were very inspired.

The Rebbetzin began preparing for Shabbos on Thursday morn-

Hadlakas Neiros

ing. She was ready for Shabbos by early Friday after-noon. There was no last-minute rush. Candle-lighting time was one of the most peaceful times of the week.

The Rebbetzin did not have silver candlesticks. She used a few metal candleholders. One day, a neighbor gave her a beautiful new silver candelabrum as a gift.

The Rebbetzin's metal candlesticks

"Thank you very much," said the Rebbetzin, "but I really prefer using my old candlesticks."

"Keep it anyway," said the generous neighbor. "If you really don't want it, please pass it along to someone else. But, of course, I would be happier if you enjoyed it yourself."

The Rebbetzin kept the boxed gift in her house for several weeks. Then she gave the present to a relative. She told her daughter Brachah that she gave away the candelabrum because (as usual) she did not want visitors to see her using an expensive silver piece. She did not want anyone to feel that they needed to copy her and get something fancy for themselves.

The candles were prepared in the *cheder hasefarim* on a high shelf covered with silver foil. Every week, one hour before the *z'man*, the Rebbetzin climbed up a ladder to reach the high shelf, and lit the Shabbos candles. When she finished lighting, she moved the ladder to another room.

Then the Rebbetzin spent a long time *davening* and talking to Hashem. She sat in a chair opposite the candles, with her hands covering her face. Soon she started crying. She *davened* for her children and grandchildren. She *davened* for hundreds of people who needed Hashem's help.

She did not even need to check a list to remember their names. "The names are etched in my heart," she told her son-in-law R' Braverman. "I feel their pain, so I remember their names and their problems."

After about 45 minutes, the Rebbetzin stopped crying. A bright smile lit up her face. "*Shabbos hi mi'liz'ok u'refuah krovah lavo,*" she said. "On Shabbos we do not cry out. May a recovery come soon!"

Then she *davened Kabbalas Shabbos.*

Over the years, the wall behind the candles got black from smoke. When the Kanievskys were having their house painted, R' Chaim asked the Rebbetzin to please tell the painters not to paint in the area of

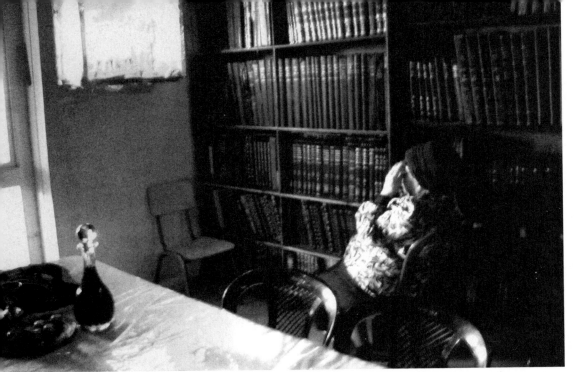

The Rebbetzin's *davening* after candle-lighting. (The photo was taken before the start of Shabbos.)

her *hadlakas neiros*. He said that it is beautiful for the house to have a wall that was blackened from the special *mitzvah* of the Rebbetzin's *hadlakas neiros*.

Every Shabbos, many guests came to eat with R' Chaim and the Rebbetzin. R' Chaim led the *zemiros* in a sweet voice. After each beautiful *niggun* he spent a few moments learning from a Gemara before starting the next *niggun*.

Shabbos Meals

The Rebbetzin served R' Chaim and each of the guests their own portion on a plate. She gave very large helpings of delicious food and always offered more.

For about 20 years, the Rebbetzin suffered from pain in her feet. Her grandson, R' Gedaliah Hongsberg, wanted to make things easier for her. He came to help her serve.

"Savta," the grandchildren asked many times, "why don't you just put big platters of food in the middle of the table? Then all the guests could help themselves. It would be much easier for you than serving the *orchim* one by one."

"No," said the Rebbetzin. "Some guests might be embarrassed to eat in front of R' Chaim if they have to serve themselves."

Besides, she liked to give every guest exactly what he liked. She remembered if her regular guests liked extra potatoes or more meat in the cholent. She knew who wanted only a small piece of kugel. She wanted each guest to feel special. And they did. The Rebbetzin's food was very tasty, and her guests happily ate the generous portions.

The Rebbetzin ate only after all her guests were served the final course.

"Please, Ima! Please, Savta!" her family begged. "Please eat something before the end of the meal!"

"Don't worry about me," she replied. "I get full by watching my guests eat!"

So many people wanted to eat with the Kanievskys that often there was not enough room for all the guests. So R' Sender Preizler started **Reservations** a phone-reservations system. People called him to find out when they could come for a Shabbos meal. He told them on which Shabbosos there were "openings" at the table. At one time there was an eight-month waiting list to eat Shabbos meals at their home!

On Shabbos, R' Sender stood at the door. "Please, only people who called in advance should come in," he said.

But some people knew another way to get invited. They would stop the Rebbetzin as she headed home from shul and ask if they could eat the *seudah* with her. Since the Rebbetzin could never say no, she would say, "Of course there is room for you! Please come in!" There was nothing her family could do to stop the Rebbetzin from bringing in her guests.

Before beginning *Kiddush* or *Bircas HaMazon,* R' Chaim would always check if the Rebbetzin was ready. *"Ima, at muchanah?"* he would

Ima Muchanah?

ask. "Ima, are you ready?" Only when the Rebbetzin answered, *"Ken, Chaim, efsher l'hatchil! — Yes, Chaim, you can start!"* would he begin.

At *Havdalah* in the later years, when more than 100 people would cram into the *cheder hasefarim*, the Rebbetzin and her granddaughters and friends would stand in the hallway and bedroom. Since R' Chaim couldn't see the Rebbetzin, he would ask his grandchildren, *"Ima muchanah?"* Only if they said that she was present and ready did he begin.

One week, the Rebbetzin was discussing an urgent question with someone in the kitchen. After asking several times whether *"Ima muchanah"* and finding out that she needed another two minutes, R' Chaim took out a *Shulchan Aruch* and started learning.

"Sabba, I can make *Havdalah* for Savta later," offered one of his grandsons.

R' Chaim looked back into his *Shulchan Aruch* and said, "I will wait for her. I'm only ready to make *Havdalah* if Savta is ready. I like making *Havdalah* for her myself."

More than 100 men in the room heard this conversation and were awed by how R' Chaim respected his wife.

One Shabbos afternoon, after making sure that R' Chaim was learning comfortably, the Rebbetzin asked her 8-year-old grandson

"Anashim Miskenim" (Unfortunate People)

Aryeh Koledetski, "Would you like to walk with me to Ramat Gan to visit my friend? She is sick in bed, and I would like to do the *mitzvah* of *bikur cholim*. It takes less than half an hour to walk there."

Aryeh loved to go places with his *savta*. She always told him the best stories while they walked together!

As they got closer to Ramat Gan, Aryeh couldn't believe his eyes. It was the middle of Shabbos afternoon, and people were driving cars!

The Rebbetzin with Aryeh (l) and Yehudah (r) Koledetski on Purim

This was the first time Aryeh had ever seen people not observing Shabbos. In Bnei Brak, as in many other religious neighborhoods in Israel, the streets are blocked on Shabbos. Only emergency vehicles pass through the streets.

"Savta," the young boy asked, "what is happening over here? Why are people being *mechalel Shabbos*?"

"Oh, Aryeh, these are unfortunate people (*anashim miskenim*) who are missing such an enjoyable and important part of life," she replied sadly. "When people visit me, I always try to tell them about the importance of Shabbos. Yet there are many people who, even when they are told about the beauty of Shabbos, don't appreciate what a special gift we have."

The Rebbetzin sighed deeply. "Whenever I see people who don't keep Shabbos, I compare them to people who are very hot and thirsty — and sitting right next to a cold drink. The beverage would cool and refresh them and they would be much better off drinking it. We can encourage people to take a cool drink, which would benefit them. If they don't sip the cold drink, they are losing a refreshing opportunity."

The Rebbetzin did not refer to these people as bad or wicked. She truly pitied them for missing out on the chance to refresh their *neshamos* with the beauty of Shabbos.

For more than 20 years, every Motza'ei Shabbos the Rebbetzin sent her Shabbos leftovers to a poor family in Bnei Brak.

Fresh Leftovers

One of the Rebbetzin's grandsons visited his grandmother one Motza'ei Shabbos and found her cooking chicken soup.

"Savta," he asked, "why are you making chicken soup now? You usually cook it on Thursday!"

She replied, "I send my Shabbos leftovers to a poor family in Bnei Brak. I always make sure to also send the leftover chicken soup. This week, some unexpected guests joined us for the Friday-night meal, so I have no soup to send. That's why I'm cooking a fresh pot now.

It's really not hard for me! Would it be right for the family to expect chicken soup and be disappointed that I didn't send any?"

She gave the contents of the entire pot — which was more than the usual amount of soup she sent — to the family that week.

CHAPTER EIGHT
Yamim Tovim

For many years, hundreds of men and women have gone to the Lederman Shul on the first night of Rosh Hashanah to wish R' Chaim and the Rebbetzin a *shanah tovah*. Of course, they would also get *berachos* from the Kanievskys in return.

L'shanah Tovah!

One year, it took more than four hours for the men and boys to greet R' Chaim in the men's section of the shul. It took about two hours for the Rebbetzin to receive the women and girls in the ladies' section.

After she finished greeting all the women, the Rebbetzin would head out of shul. But she would not go home yet. She had some important stops to make first. She would go to the houses of the widows in her neighborhood to wish them a good and healthy year. She remembered the lesson in *chessed* that she learned from her grandfather, R' Aryeh Levin. She remembered going with him, when she was a young girl, to visit the *almanos*. As an adult, she did the same *mitzvah* herself. On the last Rosh Hashanah of her life, only two weeks before her *petirah*, she visited six widows to offer them *chizuk*!

By the time R' Chaim and Rebbetzin Batsheva would finally sit down to their *seudah*, it was late. They were planning to wake up at their regular time to learn before sunrise. They would hurry to eat their Rosh Hashanah meal before midnight.

During one such meal, a grandchild asked R' Chaim and the Rebbetzin, "You are going to get up so early tomorrow morning. Why do you wish *l'shanah tovah* to so many people in one night?"

R' Chaim quickly replied, "If so many *Yidden* come to wish us the *berachah* of a good year, how can we not stand there and accept their many *berachos*?"

The Rebbetzin had a hard time fasting. Still, on Motza'ei Yom Kippur and Motza'ei Tishah b'Av, the Rebbetzin would make sure that everyone eating with them was served before she broke her fast.

Breaking the Fast

On her last Motza'ei Yom Kippur, more than 30 people came to break the fast in her house. She was not expecting so many people to come. She managed to put together enough food for all her company. Then she broke her own fast.

An inscription for the birthday of a 9-year-old girl, where the Rebbetzin wishes her a good, sweet new year

At *kapparos*

The Rebbetzin never slept in a *succah*, but she made sure to eat and drink in one.

Eating in the Succah

One grandson's *aufruf* took place on Succos. The men's *kiddush* was in the *succah*, and the women ate in the house. The *chassan* heard that his grandmother did not eat at the *kiddush*, and asked her about it.

"Well," she said, "I try not to eat outside the *succah*. Besides, I wasn't hungry at the time..."

R' Chaim cutting *aravos* (the photos were taken 30 years apart).
In the top photo, R' Chaim's son, R' Shlomo is standing at left.

R' Chaim and the Rebbetzin eating in the *succah* with grandchildren

R' Chaim inspecting
a Yemenite *esrog*

The Rebbetzin is shown a *succah* decoration that includes a photo of her husband

With the family in the *succah*

Every Hoshana Rabbah and Shavuos, R' Chaim would stay up all night learning. But first he asked the Rebbetzin for a *berachah* that he should be able to stay awake the entire night and not fall asleep while learning. The Rebbetzin would give him a long *berachah* for that, and add on many more.

Round the Clock

While R' Chaim learned in the *succah* on Hoshana Rabbah, the Rebbetzin would lie down for her regular three hours of sleep. After a short time, however, she would rise and bring cups of hot coffee into the *succah* for R' Chaim and her sons and grandsons.

"Thank you, Savta, but we can really prepare the coffee ourselves!" the grandchildren would protest.

"I know you can, but this is my way of being connected to the *minhag* of staying up all night," she would reply.

R' Chaim learning in the *succah* on the night of Hoshana Rabbah

Every night of Succos, after *Maariv*, the men in the Lederman Shul danced and sang. The Rebbetzin remained to enjoy every moment, and did not leave until the singing and dancing were done.

Simchas Torah

Simchas Torah was a highlight of the Rebbetzin's year. Even though her feet hurt, she stood and watched the *Hakafos* for hours, smiling the whole time.

This joy must have come as an "inheritance" from her father. On Simchas Torah, R' Elyashiv, who was usually very reserved, danced with great energy. He pulled other men into the circle and made sure that everyone was filled with the joy of Yom Tov.

R' Elyashiv *davening* in Tiferes Bachurim on Hoshana Rabbah

Shortly after his wedding, R' Chaim received a silver menorah from R' Aryeh Levin. It was decorated with a design of a seven-branched menorah with a lion on each side. It was the Rebbetzin's pleasure to prepare R' Chaim's menorah for each night of Chanukah.

Chanukah Lights

When the Kanievsky girls were growing up, each lit her own menorah until she became *bas mitzvah*. From then on, until she got married, R' Chaim was *motzi* her with his lighting.

On the fifth night of Chanukah, R' Chaim and the Rebbetzin hosted a *mesibah*

R' Chaim's silver menorah, a gift from R' Aryeh Levin

The Rebbetzin helping to prepare the Chanukah menorah

(gathering) for their grandchildren and distributed *d'mei Chanukah* (Chanukah *gelt*). "Does anybody know why we have the custom to give money on the fifth night of Chanukah? It's because only the fifth night cannot fall on Shabbos," R' Chaim explained.

With her grandchildren around her, the Rebbetzin would wipe away tears of gratitude and joy. Having them all come together on this night made this one of the happiest times of her year.

In 2004, someone close to R' Chaim bought him a large new menorah. R' Chaim continued to light R' Aryeh's menorah, and gave the new one to the Rebbetzin. He told her that she fulfills the *mitzvah* with his lighting, but if she wants to, she can light her menorah without a *berachah*. She decided to do so.

Dozens of women came every night to watch the Rebbetzin light her menorah about 15 minutes after R' Chaim lit his. Afterward she would sit down and give *berachos* to the many women who were there.

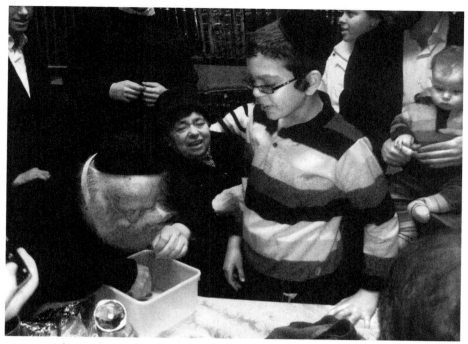

At the *mesibah* on the fifth night of Chanukah; R' Chaim and the Rebbetzin enjoy
their children and grandchildren and distribute Chanukah *gelt*.

For Purim, the Rebbetzin prepared many *mishloach manos* packages. For many years they were delivered by her children, and in later years by her grandchildren.

Purim was a time when the Rebbetzin could show how much she cared about people. This was especially true for those who did not have children, who were widowed, or who were suffering in other ways. Along with her home-baked goods and other items, she would send a loving note.

For many years, before heading to the matzah bakery to bake his matzah, R' Chaim asked the Rebbetzin for a *berachah* that the baking of the Pesach matzos should be successful.

A Blessing on the Dough

One year the matzos weren't coming out well. R' Chaim said to his son, "Perhaps the matzos didn't come out right because we forgot to get a *berachah* from Ima this year."

From then on, R' Avraham Yeshayah made sure every year to get a *berachah* from his mother before baking matzos, just in case R' Chaim forgot. He doesn't remember a year since then in which the matzos had problems.

Preparing for matzah baking

Grinding the
wheat using a
hand-operated mill

Cutting the wheat
for matzah. The youngest
son, Yitzchak Shaul
("Shuki"), is holding a
harvesting tool.

Collecting
mayim shelanu

At the
matzah bakery

The Rebbetzin never cleaned the *cheder hasefarim* while R' Chaim was learning there. She

Cleaning and Cooking for Pesach

waited for him to go learn in Kollel Chazon Ish or leave the house for another reason. Then she hurried in to clean the *cheder hasefarim* for Pesach. She never asked R' Chaim to leave the room so she could clean. She did not want to cause *bitul Torah*.

During *bedikas chametz*, R' Chaim spends a very long time on his hands and knees searching for *chametz* everywhere in his humble home. It usually takes him about three hours to complete *bedikas chametz*.

Bedikas chametz

Burning the *chametz*

The Rebbetzin did not want to start cooking for Pesach until she was sure there was no *chametz* left in the house. By the night of *bedikas chametz* the kitchen was very clean. R' Chaim came home from shul and started *bedikas chametz* in the kitchen. After he finished checking it, the Rebbetzin *kashered* the kitchen and brought down all the Pesach dishes. Then she was ready to begin cooking with her trusted helper, Miriam Cohen.

Somehow, the Rebbetzin was able to finish everything in less than 24 hours. She managed to cook for herself, for most of her children, and for other people, too. She stayed up cooking most of the night before Pesach. On Erev Pesach she was very busy and had no time to rest. But at the Seder she did not even seem tired!

On Chol HaMoed Pesach. Notice how the shelves of the regular sefarim are covered!

One year, when Erev Pesach was on Shabbos, the Rebbetzin had a dream on Friday night. She dreamed that there was *chametz* on the

A Chametzdige Dream

windowsill outside the *cheder hasefarim*. When she awoke at her usual time, she couldn't check because it was still dark outside.

After dawn she checked the windowsill, and guess what? In the exact place that she dreamed it the night before, there was a piece of bread! Somehow, the outside of the windowsill had been overlooked.

While the Rebbetzin was cooking for Pesach, she even thought about feeding people she did not yet meet.

A Welcome Pot of Cooked Potatoes

The Elbaum family moved into the Kanievskys' building the day before Pesach. They didn't *kasher* their kitchen because they were going to Yerushalayim for Yom Tov.

At 11 o'clock on Erev Pesach morning, they answered a knock on the door. There was Rebbetzin Kanievsky, with a large pot of cooked potatoes, welcoming them to the neighborhood. They thanked her for coming and introducing herself.

"But what is this pot of potatoes for?" they asked.

She replied, "I heard you were going to Yerushalayim for Pesach. I thought you might get hungry today and not have anything *kosher l'Pesach* to eat. So I brought you some cooked potatoes."

When his daughters were growing up, the Steipler (R' Chaim's father) wanted them to count *Sefiras HaOmer* with a *berachah*. Every

Counting to the End

night the Steipler was home, he asked Ahuva and Yuspa if they remembered to count. He bought a *Sefiras HaOmer* calendar and hung it up over the mirror in his daughters' bedroom. (He knew that girls like to look in the mirror!) He hoped the calendar would help them remember to count the *Omer* by themselves.

Ahuva Berman was very sick during the last few months of her life. She slept most of the time and did not always know what was going on around her. Once, Rebbetzin Kanievsky was visiting her between Pesach and Shavuos. Ahuva woke up and asked, "How many days is it in the *Omer* count today?" About a minute later she was in a deep sleep again.

When Rebbetzin Kanievsky told people this story, she said, "The way Ahuva was brought up by her father made her want to count the *Omer* even at the end of her life, when she was so sick."

Just as she did on Hoshana Rabbah, the Rebbetzin wanted to play a part in the all-night learning on Shavuos.

Coffee to Go Even though there were drinks in the Lederman Shul, the Rebbetzin would bring down cups of coffee for R' Chaim. She would wait outside the shul until she saw a man walking toward the door. Then she would rush over to him and politely ask him to deliver the coffee to R' Chaim.

The Rebbetzin brings a group from Argentina to see R' Chaim

One Erev Tishah b'Av, the Rebbetzin's neighbor noticed her standing in front of the Lederman Shul. It was very hot and humid outside,

Just Like Avraham Avinu and the Rebbetzin was not a young woman anymore.

"How can I help the *Rabbanit*?" the neighbor asked.

"I'm looking for people to invite for the afternoon meal," she answered. "I cooked for many people, and some of them did not show up."

This reminds us of Avraham Avinu after his *bris milah*, standing outside his tent in the heat of the day, looking for guests…

CHAPTER NINE
Kibbud Av Va'Eim

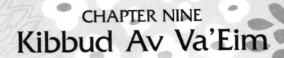

Honoring her parents was something that Batsheva did very well from when she was a young girl.

She was the oldest daughter in the family, and helped take care of her younger sisters and brothers. When she was working as a bookkeeper, she used the money she earned to help pay for things her family needed. She also did whatever had to be done so that her father, R' Elyashiv, would have more time to learn.

After Batsheva got married, she moved from Yerushalayim to Bnei Brak. Sometimes she did not see her parents for months! It was expensive to travel between the two cities, and it took a long time. Besides, R' Chaim often said that he learns better when his wife is home. Batsheva's parents understood how important it was to their daughter to help her husband learn. They understood the reason she could not visit so often.

Visiting R' Elyashiv

R' Chaim Kanievsky bringing *schach* for his parents' *succah*, delivering it in a horse-drawn wagon, on the day after Yom Kippur. The Steipler is standing at the left.

Years later, R' Chaim used to travel all over Eretz Yisrael to be *sandek* at *brisos*. When he went to Yerushalayim for a *bris*, the Rebbetzin would travel with him. While R' Chaim went to the *bris*, the Rebbetzin went to visit her parents.

R' Chaim and Batsheva greatly honored R' Chaim's parents as well. After the death of the Chazon Ish, the Steipler and Rebbetzin Miriam moved out of the house they had shared with him. R' Chaim and Batsheva invited the older Kanievskys to live with them. They made room in their small apartment, and made them feel welcome. The Steipler and his Rebbetzin lived with R' Chaim and Batsheva for six months.

Toward the end of her life, Rebbetzin Miriam was ill. Batsheva spent a lot of time helping R' Chaim's sister, Yuspa Barzam, care for her. She was not only an excellent daughter, but a wonderful daughter-in-law, as well.

On their way to Yerushalayim, where Reb Chaim was to serve as a *sandek*. The vehicle had a flat tire, and as they wait on the side of the road, R' Chaim is learning and the Rebbetzin is *davening*.

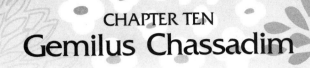

CHAPTER TEN

Gemilus Chassadim

Many people used to come to the Rebbetzin for advice and *berachos*. The house got very crowded, and sometimes noisy. A few of the people who came were mentally unwell. They would sometimes yell and behave in a way that disturbed R' Chaim, who was learning in the *cheder hasefarim*.

R' Chaim's Chessed

One day a mentally disturbed woman was standing outside the *cheder hasefarim*. She heard R' Chaim learning in a loud voice with his *chavrusa*, R' Dov. The woman stuck her head into the room and screamed, "Don't talk so loudly! You are disturbing me with your loud talking!"

R' Chaim turned to R' Dov and said, "Let's lower our voices — or maybe we can go learn in the Lederman Shul. That way, we will not bother this poor woman."

R' Chaim never asked the Rebbetzin to see fewer women in the house. He never asked her to meet the women outside, on the steps. He allowed his home to be open to everyone during the Rebbetzin's *kabbalas kahal*. (During her "*kabbalas kahal*" the Rebbetzin welcomed visitors who came to her for *berachos* and advice. R' Chaim also had a *kabbalas kahal* for men.)

The apartment where R' Chaim and the Rebbetzin lived was owned by Kollel Chazon Ish. The Kollel also owned an apartment upstairs. In 2001, the Kollel gave R' Chaim permission to use the upstairs apartment for learning. The Kanievskys were also permitted to build a second restroom. This made the situation a little easier. R' Chaim could learn undisturbed, and the Rebbetzin's visitors had more room to spread out in the apartment.

R' Chaim loves nothing more than Torah study. But sometimes, during the *kabbalas kahal*, a woman would ask the Rebbetzin a question that she could not answer by herself. So she went to discuss the problem with R' Chaim. He always listened patiently and offered advice and *berachos*. Then the Rebbetzin would hurry back to tell the woman his answer, and R' Chaim would return to his learning.

There was a family in the neighborhood that was having a problem. There were lots of children in the family, and the busy mother did

Bathing the Children

not have time to give each child a bath every day. When the father came home, he was unhappy to see that the children were not clean.

The Rebbetzin decided to help. She came to the family's house and bathed the children herself, without the father knowing. The father was not upset anymore, and everyone in the family was happier. The Rebbetzin did this *chessed* a few times a week for six whole months.

According to R' Chaim, the most positive *middah* of the Rebbetzin was her *savlanus* (patience). She was patient with all kinds of people,

Savlanus and loving and kind to them all. She was not embarrassed to do any kind of job to help anyone. She never pushed away someone who was sick or dirty or screaming. The Rebbetzin had endless patience and love for family, friends, and even strangers.

During her *kabbalas kahal*, the Rebbetzin had to deal with many colorful characters. She never laughed at anyone, and she treated everyone with respect.

When mentally unstable people sometimes screamed at the Rebbetzin, she didn't react. Once, a troubled woman poured a bucket of water over the Rebbetzin's head! The Rebbetzin was dripping wet, but she still managed to remain calm.

"Savta likes the downtrodden," R' Chaim used to tell his grandchildren.

"Yaffah" had suffered through several personal tragedies in her life and she was a very bitter woman. She visited the Rebbetzin about

The Critic twice a week. While she was there, she would often criticize the Rebbetzin in front of her family and all the other visitors.

"The line is too long. It's moving too slowly," she would say. Or, "The Rebbetzin's clothes are old. You look old fashioned."

The Rebbetzin would listen to the woman intently, then smile and hug her and kiss her before she left.

One day, the critical woman dumped a load of complaints on the Rebbetzin. After she left, Brachah asked her mother, "How can you listen to that woman always criticizing and complaining about what goes on here in our home?"

"I enjoy speaking with her," the Rebbetzin told her daughter, "and she is always welcome here. As for the criticism, I find it very helpful. Since so many women compliment me, her well-intended criticism helps balance all the compliments!"

Many people could not understand how the Rebbetzin could hug and kiss women who smelled bad or were dirty or behaved strangely.

Stronger than Her Love of Cleanliness
Rebbetzin Ahuva Berman, R' Chaim's sister, knew Batsheva since she was a young *kallah*. She remembered how neat and clean her sister-in-law always was.

"What amazes me the most about your mother," she told her niece, Brachah Braverman, "is how she hugs and kisses everyone who visits her. She was always very fussy about cleanliness and hygiene. But her love for other Jews is even stronger than her love of cleanliness!"

Many years ago, Mrs. Perel Waldman was standing by her window and saw a boy carrying a bag of garbage to the large outdoor bin. All of a sudden the boy slipped. His bag dropped out of his arms, and garbage spilled all around him. The boy did not know what to do.

Mrs. Waldman watched as the Rebbetzin, who happened to be nearby, came to help the boy. She scooped up all the garbage with her bare hands and carried it to the dumpster. It took at least three trips until she cleaned up the entire mess.

A mentally ill man came to the house to speak to R' Chaim. R' Chaim was not home. That morning, he was *sandek* at a *bris*.

A Listening (H)Ear(t)

"I don't believe he's at a *bris*!" screamed the man. "I think he's really here in the house!"

The other men who were waiting for R' Chaim tried to calm him down, but nothing worked. Then the Rebbetzin appeared.

"Have you eaten breakfast yet?" she asked kindly.

"No," admitted the man.

"Please come into the *cheder hasefarim* and eat."

She served him a full breakfast. As he was eating, R' Chaim returned home and spent a few minutes giving *chizuk* to the poor man.

"Ita" asked the Rebbetzin for a large sum of money to help pay a bill. The Rebbetzin gave her a very generous amount. Instead of thank-

Of Course I Care!

ing the Rebbetzin, Ita shouted, "You really don't care about me! If you did, you would give me more money!"

The Rebbetzin did not get offended. She did not chase Ita out of her home. "Of course I care about you!" said the Rebbetzin. "Please come back tomorrow. I will try to raise more money for you."

The Rebbetzin's grandson heard what happened. "Savta," he observed, "that lady was very rude to you. Why are you asking her to come back?"

The Rebbetzin replied, "Her behavior shows me that she is truly desperate. I will therefore try my best to put together more money for her."

There was a woman who lived in Beit Shemesh who would visit the Rebbetzin every week — for 40 years. She arrived with many shop-

Eishet Beit Shemesh ping bags full of old clothes and shoes and all sorts of junk. She collected these things from other people or found them in the garbage. She also collected food, and when her own freezer ran out of space, she put this food in the Rebbetzin's freezer. She left her bags and food in the Rebbetzin's house for several months at a time.

The Rebbetzin called her "my friend from Beit Shemesh."

When she came, the Rebbetzin always served her a hot lunch. Even though the woman smelled bad, the Rebbetzin smiled and hugged and kissed her.

"Would you like to rest for an hour or so until R' Chaim comes home from *kollel*? If you are tired, please lie down in my bed."

Sometimes the Rebbetzin had to wake her up, because R' Chaim was on his way home and she wanted to clean the room before R' Chaim arrived. When Eishet Beit Shemesh was leaving the house, the Rebbetzin would say, "I can't wait for us to spend some more time together next week!"

Sometimes the Rebbetzin asked R' Chaim if they could take Eishet Beit Shemesh along with them to a wedding. R' Chaim would tell her, "Batsheva, do as you please." The Rebbetzin was usually able to remind her to wash up before they went.

At the wedding, the Rebbetzin introduced her to many people as "my dear friend."

"Savta," one of her granddaughters once asked, "why do you always introduce Eishet Beit Shemesh to other people?"

"My friend from Beit Shemesh never got married," she replied. "Maybe one of the guests will have an idea for a *shidduch* for her."

"Shifra" was always afraid that something bad would happen to her. At least once every day she would come to the Rebbetzin for a

"You Will Not Die Today!"

berachah. "Give me a *berachah* that I will not die today!" she demanded. Sometimes she came four or five times a day. She even showed up in the middle of the night!

The Rebbetzin hugged and kissed her every time she visited. "You will live a long life!" the Rebbetzin would bless her. "You will not die today!"

"Write it down!" Shifra ordered. Then she would look at the note and scream, "No, no! You didn't write everything I told you to write!" and rip up the note. "Write it again!"

The Rebbetzin would smile and write another note. She always welcomed Shifra with love and never got angry.

"Baila" was showing signs of mental illness. She could not always tell the difference between what was real and what she was imagining.

"Try Not to Take Anything by Mistake"

She thought that people were stealing from her, even though they really weren't.

"My married children are coming to my house every day and stealing food from the refrigerator!" she complained to the Rebbetzin.

The Rebbetzin did not argue or make fun of her. Instead, with Baila standing right next to her, the Rebbetzin called each of Baila's children. She said, "I don't know which one of you is, *by mistake*, emptying your mother's refrigerator. Please be careful to ask her before you take something from her fridge. Please be extra careful not to take anything out *by mistake."*

She asked Baila to visit her every week to report whether her children were still "stealing" her food. After a while, the Rebbetzin convinced Baila to go to a special doctor for help.

A Bnei Brak woman called "Tova" wanted to behave very, very modestly. First she stopped

One Step at a Time

going out; she refused to leave her house at all.

When she was home, she wore a burqa. (A burqa is a type of clothing worn by some Arab women. It covers the entire body except the eyes.)

Family members understood that this behavior was not normal for a Jewish woman. They asked the Rebbetzin to speak to Tova. Since Tova would not go out, the Rebbetzin went to her house.

When the Rebbetzin entered, she hugged Tova. Then they had a long talk.

"Why are you behaving this way?" asked the Rebbetzin.

"I am trying to behave like Sarah Imeinu," replied Tova. "The Midrash says that she dressed in a very *tzniusdik* fashion."

"I am so impressed by how you love the *mitzvah* of *tznius*!" cried the Rebbetzin. "But, you know, we can't become as great as Sarah Imeinu in just one day.

"I have an idea. Instead of trying to be as great as Sarah Imeinu, who lived a very long time ago, first try to copy the *middos* of someone who lived closer to our time. Try to reach the *tznius* level of Sarah Schenirer.

It is very important that we Jewish women and girls become very strong in tznius, and this is a big zechus that the Shechinah should be with us and that the geulah should come quickly...

In the zechus of righteous women our parents were taken out [of Egypt], and in the zechus of righteous women and girls we will be taken out of galus.

May we be zocheh that Mashiach should come quickly.

With much love,

B. Kanievsky

"Then," the Rebbetzin concluded, "after you learn to dress and behave like Frau Schenirer, you can ask a *rav* what you can do to improve even more."

The Rebbetzin hardly ever got irritated. Her family only remembers two times that she became very upset — both times because other people were not being treated properly.

Losing Her Cool

"Binah," a girl who stuttered badly, was speaking to the Rebbetzin. Another girl — a visiting relative — was imitating Binah right in front of them. The Rebbetzin became very upset. She motioned to her relative to stop, but the girl continued her cruel imitation. "Stop embarrassing her!" the Rebbetzin cried.

Putting her arm around Binah, she brought her into her bedroom. "It must be so hard to deal with people making fun of you when you stutter," the Rebbetzin said, weeping. "I'm so sorry that you were embarrassed in my home!"

Then she helped Binah find someone to help her overcome her problem.

The second incident occurred one summer morning. A group of Israeli girls had come to *daven* in the Lederman Shul and to meet the Rebbetzin. One of the girls was walking the Rebbetzin home after *davening*. She was not dressed modestly.

A passing boy began to yell at the girl. "Shame on you!" he hollered. "Go back to Tel Aviv where you belong! How dare you come to Bnei Brak dressed like that?"

The Rebbetzin was shocked by his insults. "Who asked you?" she shouted back. "Aren't you ashamed to embarrass someone in public? Do you think you will teach a person by insulting her?

"Now I will tell you something that I never told any of the many, many people who have visited my home: you are not welcome to come and visit! If you do come to my house, I will tell you that you must leave!"

The Rebbetzin hugged and comforted the embarrassed girl, but for the rest of the day she remained sad.

The Rebbetzin knew that insulting people was not the way to teach them. She used to tell a story about her grandfather, R' Aryeh

How to Teach Right from Wrong

Levin, and how he taught someone how to behave without saying a word!

One Shabbos afternoon, R' Aryeh was walking in Yerushalayim with his son. An American visitor, holding a lit cigarette, approached him and asked for directions to his hotel.

R' Aryeh Levin

"It is hard to explain how to get there," said R' Aryeh, "but I would be happy to show you the way."

The American man spoke Yiddish to R' Aryeh. When he was younger, he had learned in a European yeshivah. R' Aryeh spoke to him about life in Europe and in the United States. He didn't say a word about smoking on Shabbos.

When they reached the hotel, the man told R' Aryeh and his son, "I don't know who you are, but I am very impressed by your self-control. It is Shabbos, and I was smoking right in front of you when we met. I know the importance of Shabbos from my yeshivah days, but have found it difficult to keep Shabbos. From now on, I will do my best to work on my self-control and not smoke again on Shabbos."

Going to the Dentist

"Judy" told the Rebbetzin that her 13-year-old granddaughter "Chumi" was in the middle of having some important dental work done. However, the girl hated the drilling so much that she refused to continue going to the dentist even though her mouth hurt.

"Please send Chumi to visit me," said the Rebbetzin.

Chumi showed up at the Rebbetzin's home and was warmly welcomed. After they chatted for a while, the Rebbetzin said, "You know, I also feel very uncomfortable sitting in the dentist's chair. But I get my teeth treated because I know it would be much worse not to go to the dentist. I really don't want my teeth to rot and fall out!

"As a matter of fact," she continued, "I have a dentist's appointment in two weeks. Would you like to come with me?"

Chumi agreed to keep the Rebbetzin company.

When they got to the dentist's office, Chumi seemed more nervous than the Rebbetzin! The dentist brought a chair into the treatment room and Chumi was allowed to watch him work on the Rebbetzin's teeth.

"I am so glad I had this work taken care of," the Rebbetzin said on the bus ride back to Bnei Brak. "It wasn't as bad as I was afraid it would be, and I'm glad you were there with me."

Then she stopped as if she had a sudden idea. "Would you like me to go with you to your next appointment?"

"Okay," said Chumi. "Thanks."

A week or two later, Chumi went to the dentist accompanied by her mother and the Rebbetzin. The Rebbetzin stayed with her until the end of the visit, telling interesting stories as the dentist worked on her teeth.

"Rebbetzin," Chumi admitted shyly when she was done, "you were right. This appointment was really not so terrible after all! Thank you for coming."

From then on, Chumi was able to go to the dentist all alone!

"Duvid" and "Esther Weingarten" and their 13-year-old daughter "Sarah," who has Down Syndrome, went to get *berachos* from the Reb-

Special Deeds for Special Needs

betzin. The Rebbetzin offered Sarah a candy, but the girl, who is shy with strangers, refused to take it.

The Rebbetzin asked, "Could you be my helper and give out candies to all the children waiting here?"

She handed Sarah a bowl of sweets to distribute.

When the girl finished giving them out, the Rebbetzin told her, "You deserve two candies because you were such a good helper!"

Sarah's parents were amazed! Sarah usually did not react to people she did not know. But the Rebbetzin was able to make her respond very quickly.

Then the Rebbetzin told Mr. and Mrs. Weingarten, "Take good care of my new friend Sarah. If you have a special-needs child in your house, it is as if you have a special *segulah* for *mazel* in your house. Children with special needs have very special *neshamos*, and it is a big *zechus* that you were given such a child to raise. The Chazon Ish used to stand up when a special-needs child entered his house, in honor of his or her lofty *neshamah*!"

A special-needs boy visiting R' Chaim

There is an interesting addition to this story.

During the meal on Shabbos Chol HaMoed Succos 5772, Sarah suddenly began talking about Rebbetzin Kanievsky and the candies she gave her. On Motza'ei Shabbos the Weingartens heard the sad news that the Rebbetzin had passed away. Sarah must have had a special feeling that made her talk about the Rebbetzin that day.

It was Thursday, and the Rebbetzin was busy cooking for Shabbos. A visitor was with her in the kitchen, and the Rebbetzin was patiently explaining about all her preparations. They spent a long time together.

A Rare Mitzvah

After the woman left, the Rebbetzin told her daughter, "Leah, I am so happy! I was able to do a special *mitzvah* which I hardly ever have a chance to do!"

"What was this special *mitzvah*?" Leah asked, puzzled.

"The lady who was here is a *giyores* [convert to Judaism]. The Torah tells us several times that it is a *mitzvah* to love converts. I spent so much time with her and gave her extra attention in order to fulfill this special *mitzvah*!"

Rabbi Yechiel Lederman and his wife built the shul in which the Kanievsky family *davened*. The Kanievskys showed their thanks in an unusual way.

Hakaras Hatov (Showing Gratitude)

After R' Yechiel Lederman passed away, his wife was afraid to sleep alone in her apartment. The Rebbetzin sent one of her daughters to keep the old lady company every night so she wouldn't be afraid. First Rutie used to go. After Rutie got married, Brachah or Deena slept over.

It was not so comfortable to sleep in her apartment. Mrs. Lederman shut all the lights by 8 o'clock. She also kept the windows closed at night, and it was very hot. But the girls went there to sleep because their mother asked them to, and they respected their mother.

The Rebbetzin knew that Deena was afraid to sleep over. She was only 8 years old when she started to go. The Rebbetzin told her daugh-

The plaque outside "The Lederman Shul," in memory of R' Yechiel Lederman and his wife.
The real name of the shul is "Beis Haknesses Chazon Ish."

ter, "Mrs. Lederman is an *almanah*. She is old and cannot stay home alone. Every minute that you spend in Mrs. Lederman's apartment, you get a *mitzvah*. Even when you are asleep, you are getting *mitzvos*. So even if you are a little afraid at the beginning, isn't it worth it to get so many, many *mitzvos*? "

After hearing these words, Deena agreed to go right away.

The Rebbetzin did not want Mrs. Lederman to feel as if the Kanievskys were doing her a favor. So she said, "Thank you so much for allowing my daughters to sleep in your apartment! You know that we have a large family and a small apartment. Thanks to your *chessed*, we now have more room!"

The Rebbetzin thanked her so many times that Mrs. Lederman truly believed that she was doing a favor to the Kanievskys, and not the other way around!

A few years later, Mrs. Lederman fell on the sidewalk and had to go to the hospital. The doctors would not let her leave unless she had someone to take care of her.

"I'll take care of her!" Rebbetzin Kanievsky offered. "Please bring her to my house."

Mrs. Lederman spent several months in the Kanievskys' home. She slept in the front hall, and the Rebbetzin was her nurse. Then the doctor sent her to a nursing home, where she spent the rest of her life.

None of the Kanievskys were paid for taking care of Mrs. Lederman; at least, they did not get paid money in this world. But the *mitzvos* they got cannot be counted!

Sometimes parents wanted to send their young children to *cheder*, but were told the school was full. Or a girl was not accepted to high

Letters of Recommendation

school or seminary, or a *bachur* was having trouble getting into yeshivah. Then the parents or the students would go to the Rebbetzin and ask for a *berachah* to get into the school they wanted.

The Rebbetzin always gave a warm *berachah*. Sometimes she wrote a letter of recommendation to the principal or *rosh yeshivah*,

At the wedding of R' Shlomo Kanievsky; (l-r) the Steipler, R' Chaim, the *chassan*, the *mechutan* R' Meir Honigsberg

or even visited in person. Many students got accepted because of the Rebbetzin's efforts.

One day the Rebbetzin heard two pieces of good news: Her son, R' Shlomo, had accepted a certain boy into his yeshivah, and R' Shlomo's son was getting engaged that night. She said to R' Shlomo, "I am so happy that my grandson is getting engaged! And I am even happier that you accepted this *talmid* into your yeshivah!"

"Shuie H." was a boy from Haifa who was a very average student. Right before the entrance exams for *yeshivos gedolos* were scheduled

Now She'll Be Able to Sleep

to take place, Shuie's mother passed away.

Of course, Shuie did not do well on his entrance exams. Not a single yeshivah accepted him.

Shuie's father heard about how the Rebbetzin worked so hard to get boys into yeshivos. "Mr. H." decided to visit the Rebbetzin.

"My son is suffering so much from the death of his mother," he cried. "And now, to top it all off, he was not accepted to any yeshivah!"

The Rebbetzin found out that Shuie was a very religious young man, but was not a top student.

"I must get this orphan into a good yeshivah!" she decided. "He is blessed with *yiras Shamayim* and he is a hard worker. These are even more important than being born smart."

She sent letters to a few yeshivos, but Shuie still was not accepted. For the next week she asked everyone she knew if they could help get him into a yeshivah.

One *rosh yeshivah* was very impressed with the Rebbetzin's efforts to help an orphan whom she had never met. He agreed to accept Shuie as a *talmid*.

The night Shuie was accepted, Mr. H. made a special trip from Haifa to Bnei Brak to thank the Rebbetzin. He arrived at about 11:30 p.m.

Shuie's father was told that the Rebbetzin was resting. He would not be able to speak to her that night. So he waited on line for R' Chaim, who was still seeing people, and told him the news.

"*Baruch Hashem!*" said R' Chaim. "May you have much *nachas* from this son and from the rest of your children! Now I will go and tell the Rebbetzin the good news!"

R' Chaim left the long line of people who were waiting to see him, and hurried into the bedroom. Three minutes later he came out. With a big smile, he told the boy's father, "The Rebbetzin is crying tears of joy for you and your son. She wanted to come out of bed to wish you *mazel tov*, but I convinced her to stay in bed. She needs to get some rest."

At the end of R' Chaim's *kabbalas kahal*, his son in-law asked, "Why did you wake Ima? Couldn't the news wait until morning?"

"You don't understand," replied R' Chaim. "For the last week Ima has not been able to sleep at night. She keeps waking up and crying and *davening* for the orphan from Haifa. Now that she knows the boy has been accepted into a yeshivah, she will be able to sleep properly for the first time in more than a week!"

Rebbetzin Kanievsky was very generous and loving to her family. She prepared freshly squeezed juices for a great-nephew who needed

Savta's Grocery Stores

to drink these juices for his health. She bought extra food and sent it home with her married children and grandchildren. And, of course, she sent them delicious salads, kugels, fish, challos, chicken, and cake for Shabbos. Soon the family had a joke. They called the Kanievsky home "Savta's *makolet* (grocery)."

Her grandson, R' Aryeh Koledetski, came to learn with R' Chaim. When he was ready to leave, the Rebbetzin handed him a bag of food to take home.

"Savta," he said, "I came to learn with Sabba, not to get food for my family!"

The Rebbetzin smiled. "There is no such thing as coming to our house and leaving empty-handed!" she said. "Enjoy the food!"

But where did the Rebbetzin buy her food?

For many years the Rebbetzin shopped in the Vizhnitz Grocery, a few blocks away from her house. Then another *makolet* opened up next door. Where should she shop now? If she switched to the new Gross Grocery, the owner of the Vizhnitz Grocery might feel bad. But if she continued to walk 10 minutes to the Vizhnitz Grocery, the owner of the *makolet* next door would wonder why she didn't shop there!

She solved the problem by taking turns and shopping in both stores!

The Rebbetzin loved to attend the school events of her grandchildren and great-grandchildren. One time she couldn't make it to her

Graduations and Siddur Parties

granddaughter Chayala's graduation. The Rebbetzin wrote a letter to the principal and teachers, thanking them for all their efforts and blessing them. She signed the letter "the *savta* of Chayala, and the *savta* of them all."

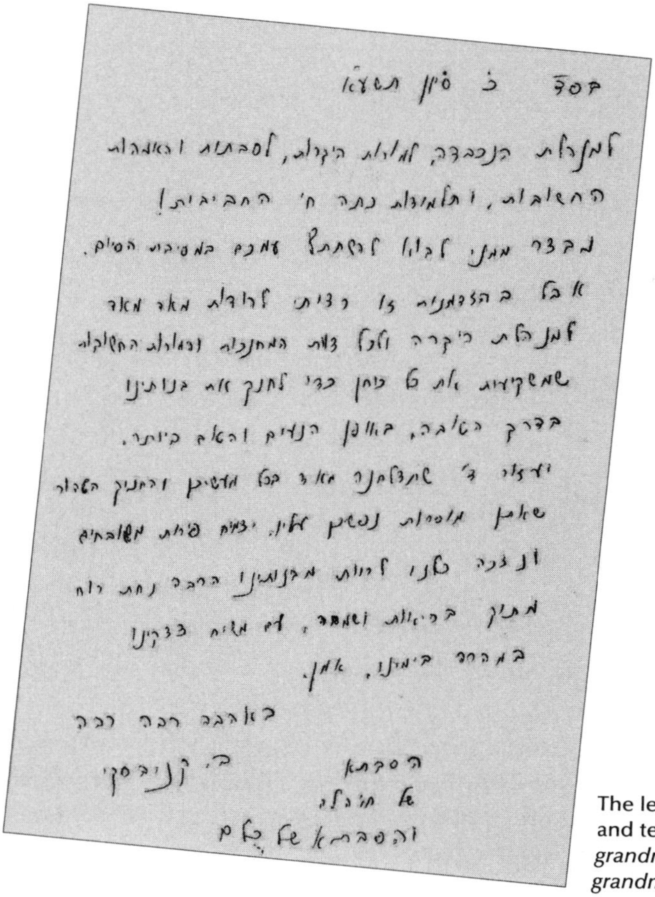

בס"ד כ' סיון מאיר

[Hebrew handwritten letter — partially legible]

The letter to Chayala's principal and teachers, signed "The grandmother of Chayala and the grandmother of them all."

"Ima, why did you sign as the grandmother of the whole class? Only Chayala is your granddaughter," asked her puzzled daughter-in-law Sarah.

"I feel close to everyone in the class, because they are the class-mates of my dear granddaughter!" she replied. "I want to show them all how much I love them!"

Another time, the Rebbetzin's daughter Deena Epstein was getting ready to go to her little daughter's *Siddur* party. "Please wait for me!" the Rebbetzin called out. "I am also going!"

On the way, the Rebbetzin admitted, "You know, I am really not feeling so well today. But I don't want Miriam to be upset that I went to her older sisters' *Siddur* parties and not hers. That's why I'm pushing myself to go."

Devorah came from a family that did not keep *mitzvos*. She wanted to become religious, so she went to Bnei Brak to study in a seminary for *baalos teshuvah*. It was not easy for her to make so many changes to her life all at once.

Warm Hands, Warm Heart

That winter, Devorah *davened* in the Lederman Shul for two days. The Rebbetzin's sharp eyes noticed her. During *davening*, the Rebbetzin took her coat and put it over Devorah's shoulders. "My dear daughter," she said, "you look so cold." The Rebbetzin held on to Devorah's icy hand as she finished *davening*. Then she invited her over for breakfast.

As she ate, Devorah began to weep. "It's so hard for me to get used to being religious," she sobbed, "even though I really want to!"

The Rebbetzin listened patiently. "Take one step at a time," she told the young woman. "Don't try to change everything at once."

Years later, Devorah became a *madrichah* (leader) who worked with other *baalos teshuvah*. She began sending her students to speak to the Rebbetzin.

"The Rebbetzin's warm hands on that icy cold morning warmed my heart and helped me become religious," she said.

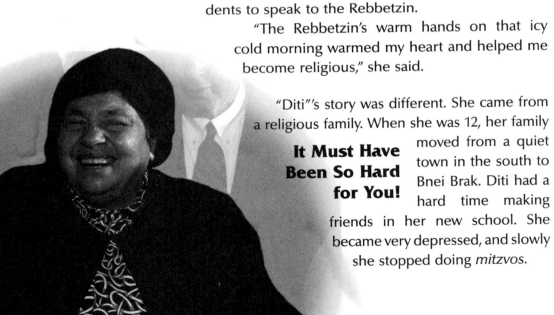

"Diti"'s story was different. She came from a religious family. When she was 12, her family moved from a quiet town in the south to Bnei Brak. Diti had a hard time making friends in her new school. She became very depressed, and slowly she stopped doing *mitzvos*.

It Must Have Been So Hard for You!

A few years later, she decided to go speak to the Rebbetzin. She told the Rebbetzin about her childhood.

"When I was 13 years old," she explained, "I started out in a new school. Nobody paid attention to me or wanted to be my friend. I still feel so sad when I think about it."

The Rebbetzin stood up and began hugging her and crying with her.

Finally somebody understands me and cares for me! thought the young woman.

Two weeks later, she returned for another visit. Again, the Rebbetzin listened to her describe her pain. "It must have been so hard for you!" the Rebbetzin said. Diti could see that the Rebbetzin understood exactly how she felt.

After a while, Diti returned to *Yiddishkeit*. She moved to Yerushalayim, got married, and became a mother. She remained close to the Rebbetzin and came to help her two days every month — just to say thank you.

CHAPTER ELEVEN

Giving Tzedakah

R' Chaim Kanievsky has written many *sefarim*. One of them is called *Orchos Yosher*. R' Chaim and the Rebbetzin agreed to give all the money they earned from selling this *sefer* to *tzedakah*. This money was put into a separate container and only used for *tzedakah*.

During the Rebbetzin's *kabbalas kahal*, people sometimes gave her money and said, "Please give this to people who need it." She made sure to give out the money that same day.

The Rebbetzin was able to figure out who needed help, even when they did not ask for it.

"R' Yossel" was a *talmid chacham*. He came to talk in learning to R' Chaim. The Rebbetzin noticed that his clothing was old and worn out. She took him aside and handed over a wad of cash.

"You are so lucky that you can study Torah all day!" she said. "Here's a little something to help you out."

Before he could say anything, she quickly pulled out pictures of her grandchildren and started telling a story about them. She did not give R' Yossel a chance to refuse the gift.

Sometimes she did the opposite. "Would you like to see pictures of my grandchildren?" she would ask. While the visitor politely looked at the pictures, she would slip him or her some money that she had received that day.

The Rebbetzin took great care not to embarrass people when she gave them *tzedakah*.

There was one needy *talmid chacham* who came every Friday morning to pick up a check. The Rebbetzin had the check prepared for him every week for 40 years. If anyone else was around when he came, she made sure to give him the envelope when nobody was watching.

One night, in her later years, the Rebbetzin was in terrible pain. She didn't have enough strength to see people that evening. As her

Maybe She Is Hungry

doctor had ordered, she was resting in bed.

At about 11:00 someone knocked at the door. Her grandson Aryeh Koledetski opened the door to a poor woman who was collecting *tzedakah*.

Aryeh went to the Rebbetzin. "Savta," he said, "there is a woman at the door collecting *tzedakah*."

"Please give her 100 shekelim,"(Shekalim is the name of the money used in Eretz Yisroel.) said the Rebbetzin. Aryeh did what his grandmother asked.

But then he heard the Rebbetzin calling him. "Aryeh, Aryeh! Please come back!" When he returned to his *savta's* room, she was standing near her bed with another 100 shekelim in her hand.

"I cannot see this woman because I am weak and must follow my doctor's orders," she said. "But I am worried that maybe she is hungry. Please take 100 shekelim more, hurry outside, and give her the additional money. Tell her to use it to buy food."

Then the Rebbetzin went back to bed.

Every Tuesday and Friday after the sunrise *minyan*, "Mrs. Levi" received 400 *shekalim* from the Rebbetzin. For the last five years before her *petirah*, the Rebbetzin would walk over to Mrs. Levi after *davening* and slip an envelope into her pocketbook.

One Friday morning, Mrs. Levi left the shul before the Rebbetzin could get to her. Later that morning, the Rebbetzin sent one of her granddaughters with the money to Mrs. Levi's house.

"I am so upset with myself for not noticing that Mrs. Levi left the shul while I was talking to some other women!" the Rebbetzin told her assistant. "Because of me, poor Mrs. Levi had to wait a few extra hours to get her money!"

That was the last Friday morning of Rebbetzin Kanievsky's life.

CHAPTER TWELVE
Tefillah and the Shul

The Rebbetzin had a tremendous love of *tefillah*. She also loved her shul. "It is my honor to clean the area around the ladies' entrance," she told her friend as she bent down to pick up some garbage.

Inside and Out

In her younger years, the Rebbetzin scrubbed the floors of the *ezras nashim* every Friday afternoon. Sometimes her daughters or daughters-in-law would help. They wanted to make the *beis hamidrash* sparkle for Shabbos.

Even as a single girl, Batsheva *davened* at home three times a day and said *Tehillim*. After she got married, she continued *davening* three *tefillos* and saying *Tehillim* at home.

Davening With or Without a Minyan

When her youngest son, Shuki (Yitzchak Shaul), was 12, he no longer needed the Reb-

R' Chaim with Shuki at Shuki's *bar mitzvah*

betzin to watch him at home. The Rebbetzin then began *davening* all three *tefillos* with a *minyan*. After a while, Mrs. Ayala Nachumi joined her. Slowly, other ladies came to join the Rebbetzin and Mrs. Nachumi in the *ezras nashim* at sunrise.

After a while, the *ezras nashim* had more than 100 women at the *netz* (sunrise) *minyan*. The women would say *berachos* one by one as the others answered *amen*.

After *Shacharis*, the Rebbetzin tried to get home before R' Chaim in order to serve him his breakfast. But more and more women were starting to approach her in shul for *berachos* and advice. So she taught Shuki how to prepare cooked eggs and to cut up tomatoes and cucumbers for R' Chaim's breakfast.

The Rebbetzin made sure to get home before R' Chaim finished eating. "The Rav is waiting for me," she would tell the women. "I'll be back soon."

No matter where she was, the Rebbetzin made sure to *daven* on time. She always got to shul early.

Always on Time
Even at family *s'machos*, she would stay on the ladies' side of the *mechitzah* and *daven Maariv* with the *minyan*. Sometimes other women joined her.

The Rebbetzin was in the hospital and R' Shlomo was spending the night at his mother's side. Every few minutes she woke up and looked at her watch. Finally, a little after 2:00 a.m., she washed *netilas yadayim*.

"Ima, you're in the hospital! Please try to rest!" R' Shlomo begged.

"I'm fine, really, and I feel the need to *daven*," she answered. Only after saying *Tehillim* and *Nishmas Kol Chai* was she able to rest again.

If people were waiting on line to see her at home, she invited them to *daven* with her in the Lederman shul when it was time for *Minchah* or *Maariv*.

"Let's *daven* to Hashem together," she would say, "and He will answer us."

Even as a child, the Rebbetzin believed strongly in the power of *tefillah*.

The Power of Tefillah

When Batsheva Elyashiv was 8 years old, her grandmother, Rebbetzin Tziporah Chana Levin, became very sick.

Batsheva was at home on 10 Chanan Street in Meah Shearim, *davening* and saying *Tehillim* for her grandmother. In the middle of the night, the little girl finally fell asleep with the *sefer Tehillim* held tightly in her hands.

Batsheva had a frightening dream. She was at her grandmother's bedside in the Mishkenot neighborhood, reciting *Tehillim*. Suddenly, a frightening figure dressed in white shrouds started pulling at Rebbetzin Tziporah Chana's bed. Still reciting *Tehillim*, Batsheva grabbed the bed and pulled back. The man in shrouds was bigger and stronger than she was, but she would not let go. He pulled and she pulled.

Finally, she stopped saying *Tehillim* and screamed at the scary intruder. "Let go of my *savta* right now! You have no right to be near her! Go away! Now!" The creature disappeared.

Batsheva woke up with her worried mother at her side.

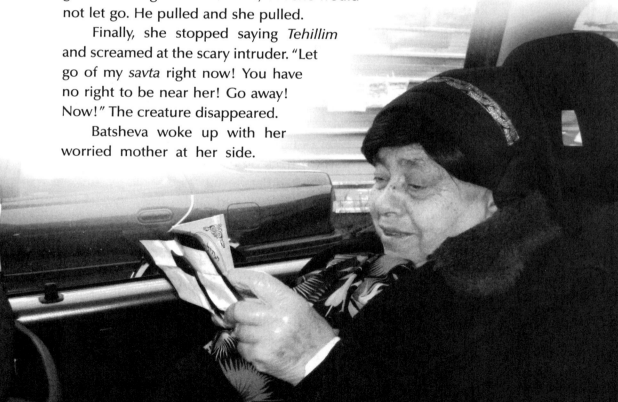

"What happened, Batsheva? Why were you screaming?" Trembling, Batsheva told her mother about her dream.

Rebbetzin Elyashiv hurried to Mishkenot to check on her mother's condition. At the house, she found her father, R' Aryeh, talking to the doctor. Just 20 minutes earlier — when Batsheva was screaming at the intruder —Rebbetzin Levin had passed a crisis. *Baruch Hashem*, she was now out of danger.

When the doctor left, R' Aryeh turned to his daughter Shaina Chaya. "What brought you here just now, when Ima's condition was critical?"

Rebbetzin Elyashiv told her father about the dream and the screaming. R' Aryeh said, "It was Batsheva's special *neshamah* and pure *tefillos* that saved Ima's life."

The next morning after *davening*, R' Aryeh went to the Elyashiv home to tearfully thank Batsheva for her *tefillos*.

Rebbetzin Levin lived 10 more years. She passed away about three months after her granddaughter Batsheva married R' Chaim Kanievsky.

A few years after Rebbetzin Levin's illness, the family was tested again.

Shoshana Aliza Elyashiv became very sick and was sent to the hospital. The family took turns sitting with the 13-year-old girl as her condition got worse.

One night, it was Batsheva's turn to stay with her younger sister. A doctor came into the room to check on his patient.

"How is my sister doing?" asked Batsheva.

The doctor shuffled his feet and looked at the floor. "Well," he finally said, "I really don't think that she will get better. I think your family should prepare for the worst."

Batsheva was very upset. It was only a year since her baby sister Rivkah had been killed by a Jordanian shell. She hurried home and repeated the doctor's words.

R' Elyashiv closed his *Gemara*, opened his *Tehillim*, and began pleading with Hashem to spare the life of his daughter. For the next

R' Chaim with R' Yitzchak Zilberstein (R). R' Michel Yehudah Lefkowitz is in the background.

hour, he and his wife, Shaina Chaya, with Batsheva at their side, *davened* to Hashem.

After an hour, R' Elyashiv gently put down his *Tehillim*. "Now I will continue learning," he calmly told his daughter, and turned back to his *Gemara*. "Hashem will help. Everything will work out for the best."

The next morning, Shoshana Aliza was a little better. About three weeks later, she was sent home from the hospital in excellent condition.

"The tears and *tefillos* of my father and mother added 50 years onto my sister's life!" Rebbetzin Kanievsky said many years later, during Shoshana Aliza Zilberstein's *shivah* in 1999.

"I *davened* so hard, but my *tefillos* were not answered!"

When people don't get what they *daven* for, they sometimes think

No Prayer Goes Unanswered

that Hashem wasn't listening.

After the Rebbetzin's brother-in-law, R' Yosef Yisraelzon, passed away, someone asked the Rebbetzin, "How could it be that he did not get better? So many people *davened* so hard for him to get better!"

The Rebbetzin replied, "We don't understand what Hashem does, but a *tefillah* never goes unanswered. The prayers will be a merit for R' Yosef's soul, and a *zechus* for other people, that in the merit of our *tefillos*, no tragedies should happen to them."

The Rebbetzin used to say a *dvar Torah* about *tefillos* being answered:

One More Tefillah

Moshe Rabbeinu wanted so badly to go to Eretz Yisrael. He davened so many times, but Hashem did not allow him to enter the Holy Land. It is brought down that if Moshe Rabbeinu would have davened just once more for his heart's desire, Hashem would have agreed to his request.

This shows us that every single tefillah counts, and one never knows which tefillah will be answered and when it will be answered. If someone sees that he prayed and was not answered, he should pray again!

Returning from *davening* at *kivrei tzaddikim*

The Power to Heal

'When people were sick, the Rebbetzin advised them to go to a doctor. But she believed that even if a doctor said that a patient would not get better, *tefillah* could change this.

"Penina" was the mother of 11 children. Her fifth child was getting married in a little over a month. But Penina got very sick and was told that she had only one month to live.

"What should we do?" the family asked the Rebbetzin. "Should we make the wedding earlier so that Penina will be able to attend?"

The Rebbetzin asked R' Chaim this question. "Make the wedding earlier," he answered, "but don't give up hope and keep on *davening*."

"I am *davening* for your mother's speedy recovery!" the Rebbetzin would tell Penina's daughter in shul. "Tell your mother not to give up. *Tefillah* can change the worst diagnosis!"

With Hashem's help, Penina got better. Not only did she celebrate her fifth child's wedding, but she was also at the weddings of two more of her children!

The Rebbetzin *davened* at least once a day for each of her grand-children and great-grandchildren. She also *davened* for many other people besides her family.

Davening for Others

People came to the Rebbetzin and asked her to *daven* for them. "Their names, their challenges, their needs, and their problems are etched in my heart," she explained to her family.

Miriam Cohen's mother visited the Rebbetzin one year, before Rosh Hashanah. "I have your entire family in mind during my *tefillos*," the Rebbetzin said. And to "prove" it, she recited the names of 20 members of the Cohen family!

Even though the Rebbetzin's *berachos* became famous, and crowds of people came to her for blessings, she asked people to *daven* for her. When she didn't feel well, she asked *roshei yeshivah* — as well as her grandchildren — for *berachos* to feel better. She asked her children to have her in mind in their own *tefillos*.

When a *kallah* would visit on her wedding day, the Rebbetzin would give her a *sefer*. Inside, she wrote beautiful *divrei berachah* (blessings). She posed with the *kallah* for pictures and showered her with blessings. Then she asked the *kallah* to have her in mind when she was *davening* under the *chuppah*.

"So many people with *tzaros* come to me for *berachos*," she said. "Since the *tefillos* of a *kallah* under the *chuppah* are heard, please *daven* that Hashem should answer my *tefillos* and help them all."

The Rebbetzin always agreed to *daven* for others. Sometimes she told them, "If you *daven* also, the *tefillah* will be stronger, because the

The Rebbetzin with the twins born to a couple who were married
for 16 years before having children

prayers of two people are stronger than the prayers of one." In this way
the Rebbetzin strengthened the *tefillah* of others.

During her last months, the Rebbetzin started wearing a jacket over
her regular clothing in the hot Bnei Brak weather. When her daughter
Brachah Braverman asked about the extra garment, she explained, "It's
a jacket for *davening*. I decided to dress for *davening* with more *tznius*
as a *segulah* for someone who needs a big *yeshuah*."

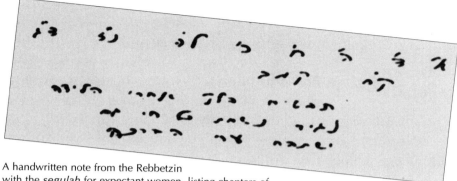

A handwritten note from the Rebbetzin
with the *segulah* for expectant women, listing chapters of
Tehillim to be recited daily and to accept, *bli neder*, to recite *Nishmas* after the birth

Since she was a young girl, the Rebbetzin was careful about how she *davened*. She always said *Bircas HaMazon* from a *Siddur*, and would

Being Careful with Davening

recite it slowly and concentrate on every word. She did the same with the *berachah* of *Asher Yatzar*. She hung up signs with the words of the *berachah* in two places in her house, and always said this blessing while reading from a sign or a *Siddur*. Sometimes she told a sick person that saying *Asher Yatzar* with concentration would help him or her get better.

Another *tefillah* that was very dear to the Rebbetzin was *Nishmas Kol Chai*. She said it at least once every day. She told people to say this prayer when they needed help from Hashem. She also told them to say it when their problem was solved or their prayers were answered. Some women came to the Rebbetzin and said *Nishmas* in front of her.

Older single girls used to come to the Rebbetzin for advice. "What can I do to help find my *basherte*?" they would ask.

Daven Regularly
"*Daven* at least *Shacharis* every day, and say *Perek* 121 of *Tehillim* at the end of *Shemoneh Esrei*," she replied. "I don't know if I can *daven Shacharis* daily. I have to be at work early in the morning!" some of them responded.

"Whenever someone does something difficult, it is like a *korban*, a sacrifice," the Rebbetzin explained. "Hashem appreciates a *korban*. It is very important not to miss even one day of *Shacharis*."

Then she would tell a story about R' Meir Shapiro, who started the *Daf Yomi* program.

> When R' Meir was a young child, his mother hired a rebbi to study with him. When she ran out of money to pay him, she pawned her jewelry.
>
> One day there was a big snowstorm and the rebbi didn't come. Meir's mother cried for a very long time that morning.
>
> Young Meir tried to make his mother feel better. "I'm sure the rebbi will come tomorrow and we will make up what we missed today," he said.
>
> "Meir," she replied, "it is important that learning takes place every day. Tomorrow's tomorrow, but you are missing your learning today. That's why I'm so sad."
>
> R' Meir Shapiro later gave his mother part of the credit for his idea of learning Daf Yomi to make every day count.

CHAPTER THIRTEEN
Hachnasas Orchim

R' Chaim and the Rebbetzin always had lots of guests on Shabbos and Yom Tov. Sometimes they did the inviting, and sometimes people — even strangers — invited themselves.

At the Lederman Shul one Friday night, a *bachur* named "Mutty" asked one of the Kanievsky sons if he could eat the Friday-night meal with them.

"We Will Make Room!"

"I'm sorry," he answered, "the night meal is full, but you may come for the Shabbos-day meal."

"I can't get up so early on Shabbos to *daven* at the sunrise *minyan*!" Mutty complained.

But he did not take no for an answer. He just walked into the house and sat down at the table.

One of the grandchildren was very upset by Mutty's rude behavior. "Savta," he asked, right in front of Mutty, "what do we do if we invite someone for tomorrow and he insists on coming tonight, and there is no room tonight for him?"

With two of her grandchildren who are sitting in the Steipler's chair

The Rebbetzin smiled sweetly and replied, "Don't you know that by us the door is always open for everyone who wants to come in? Of course he can stay! We will make room."

During the Friday-night and Shabbos-day meals, the door to the Kanievsky house was always open. Visitors would simply walk in to ask

Open Doors

advice, discuss their learning, or just wish a *Gut Shabbos*. R' Chaim and the Rebbetzin welcomed everyone. If the visitor came with a child, the Rebbetzin offered candies or taffies.

The Rebbetzin's grandchildren called her and R' Chaim "Savta Rashbam" and "Sabba Rashbam" because they lived on Rechov Rash-bam.

Savta Rashbam

By the time she passed away, the Rebbetzin had close to 60 married grandchildren and great-grandchildren. In fact, she even became a great-great-grandmother during her lifetime!

The children enjoyed their *savta's* delicious cooking. The Rebbetzin always tried to make each grandchild's favorite foods

when he or she came to visit. The Rebbetzin loved to have her grandchildren visit. They often came for *seudah shelishis*. Sometimes they came early, so the Rebbetzin did not have a chance to rest on Shabbos afternoon. But she did not mind; having them over was worth missing her rest.

The Kanievskys' bedroom had some very strange items in it. There were two refrigera-

Caring for the Visitors' Children

tors and a freezer, and also a crib. The crib was used when the Rebbetzin babysat for her grandchildren. Even after she stopped babysitting, the crib remained in her bedroom.

"Ima, there are so many things in this bedroom, and hardly any room at all! Can I take out the crib to make more room?" R' Avraham Yeshayah asked his mother.

The Rebbetzin replied, "*Chas v'shalom*! It is still used today. When I have a visitor with a baby waiting on line to see me, I offer the crib in our bedroom so that the baby can rest."

Many children came with their parents to see the Rebbetzin. She always gave out candies and taffies with a big smile.

"Here," she would say, "take some more to share with your brothers and sisters!"

The Rebbetzin always had lots of food in her refrigerators and freezer. Everyone who walked in was allowed to take whatever they

Everything Is for Everybody

wanted. Sometimes the Rebbetzin gave away so much food to family members, guests, and poor people that there was almost nothing left for her and R' Chaim!

One grandson started to put stickers on some of the food and on one bottle of R' Chaim's diet grapefruit drink. The stickers said "Reserved for the Rav and *Rabbanit*." Sometimes even this didn't help. People did not notice the stickers, or they ignored them. Besides, the Rebbetzin did not like to tell people not to take food. "Everything is for everybody," she would say.

One of the people who always took food was "Milka." She lived nearby, and would empty out most of the Rebbetzin's refrigerator. She even took home-made meals and cakes and cookies.

"Please don't take any more food," someone from the Kanievsky family finally said to her.

"But the *Rabbanit* gave me permission to feed my family from her refrigerator!" Milka answered.

The relatives begged the Rebbetzin not to allow Milka to take the cooked food. The Rebbetzin replied, "Should Milka and her family starve? I always make sure there's enough food for Abba and me. My refrigerator and food are public property."

Finally, someone arranged for Milka to get *tzedakah* every month. The money was enough for her to feed her family, and she stopped helping herself to the Rebbetzin's food.

"Mrs. Scheiner," an older woman who was very poor, often came to the Rebbetzin's house, and the Rebbetzin would serve her a delicious hot meal.

A Good Deal for a Meal

After she finished eating, Mrs. Scheiner would give the Rebbetzin about 10 *shekalim* (which was not very much money) to "pay" for the meal. The Rebbetzin took the money to make the poor lady feel good.

When Mrs. Scheiner was ready to leave, the Rebbetzin would hand her an envelope with 100 *shekalim* inside.

"I don't need *tzedakah*!" Mrs. Scheiner would say proudly.

"*Tzedakah*? Oh, no, you are mistaken! Someone just asked me to give you this envelope, and here it is!"

One time, a visitor from America noticed a plate of freshly baked cookies in the Rebbetzin's kitchen.

Just One Cookie

"May I please take one cookie back to America for my wife?" he asked. "She would be so delighted to have a cookie from the Rebbetzin."

The Rebbetzin immediately emptied the entire plate of cookies into a bag and gave the bag to the surprised visitor. Then she said, "Next week is Rosh Hashanah. I'm sure your wife would also enjoy a honey cake!" And she handed him one of her home-made cakes!

On the last Erev Yom Kippur of her life, the Rebbetzin told her daughter, "Leah, I bought myself a treat!"

The Rebbetzin's Treat

Leah was surprised. "What did you buy?" she asked.

The Rebbetzin showed her two bottles of grape juice. "It is a *mitzvah* to eat on Erev Yom Kippur," she explained, "and I want to be strong when I fast. So I asked one of the grand-children to buy me two bottles of grape juice."

"But Ima, you have many bottles of grape juice on the porch and in the refrigerator. Why did you send someone to buy more bottles?"

The Rebbetzin replied, "The bottles on the porch and in the refrigerator belong to everyone. They are not just mine."

About two hours later, Leah saw only one bottle of grape juice in the kitchen. It was almost empty.

"Where is the second bottle?" she asked her mother.

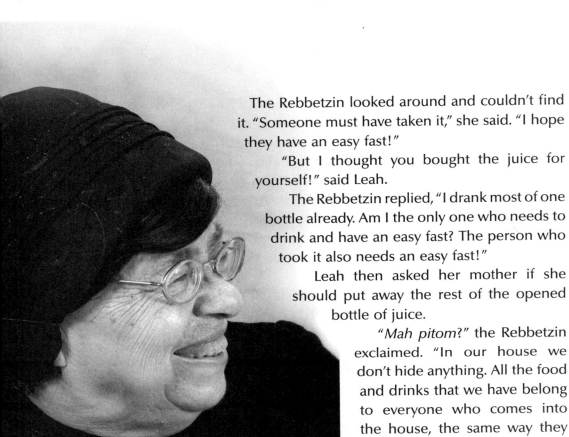

The Rebbetzin looked around and couldn't find it. "Someone must have taken it," she said. "I hope they have an easy fast!"

"But I thought you bought the juice for yourself!" said Leah.

The Rebbetzin replied, "I drank most of one bottle already. Am I the only one who needs to drink and have an easy fast? The person who took it also needs an easy fast!"

Leah then asked her mother if she should put away the rest of the opened bottle of juice.

"*Mah pitom?*" the Rebbetzin exclaimed. "In our house we don't hide anything. All the food and drinks that we have belong to everyone who comes into the house, the same way they belong to us."

CHAPTER FOURTEEN
Bikur Cholim

It is a big *mitzvah* to visit someone who is sick. This *mitzvah* is called *bikur cholim*.

How do you do this *mitzvah*? You visit the patient, talk to the person, and listen when he or she talks, and then you wish a *"refuah sheleimah!"* Of course, you should also *daven* for the person to get well.

The Rebbetzin often visited sick people. If one of her married children or grandchildren was not feeling well, she would stop by to check up on them. She would also visit friends and neighbors in the hospital. While she was visiting them, she would stop by strangers' rooms to cheer them up!

R' Chaim visiting a patient in the hospital

The Steipler

Whenever the doctors and nurses in a hospital heard that the Rebbetzin was visiting, they came running to her for *berachos*. First she would tell them, "Your work is so important! You have the chance to take care of Hashem's children. This is not just a regular job!" She would then give *berachos* to the staff.

When the Rebbetzin visited the sick, she saw that most patients did everything the doctor told them to do. Some needed to take

Run for Your Life!

medicine. Some needed to rest. Some needed to exercise. And they did. But other patients had a harder time following doctors' orders, and needed a little encouragement. Those were the patients to whom the Rebbetzin told this funny true story that happened when the Steipler was a *talmid* in the Novardok Yeshivah.

> *"Mendy" and "Zalman" were walking in the marketplace of a town in Europe. Suddenly, Mendy turned very pale. "There's a police officer down the road," he gasped, "and he's coming toward us! I did not yet register with the police. If the officer catches me without papers, he can throw me in jail for a week!"*
>
> *"I'll help you out," offered Zalman. He began jogging away from the policeman.*
>
> *The policeman was suspicious. Why was this Jewish boy running away? "Hey, boy! Come here!" he yelled. When Zalman did not turn around, the officer began to chase him. Meanwhile, Mendy ran back to yeshivah.*

R' Chaim visiting a patient in the hospital

Soon the angry Ukrainian policeman caught up with Zalman. "Papers!" he barked.

Zalman pulled out his documents and showed them to the policeman.

"Why were you running away from me?" asked the officer, as he handed back the papers.

"I wasn't running away from you," answered Zalman. "My doctor told me that I have to exercise. I was jogging for my health."

"But when you turned around and saw me running after you, why didn't you stop?" asked the policeman.

The bachur replied, "I thought that maybe your doctor told you the same thing — that you should jog for your health. So of course I didn't stop. I thought you were following doctors' orders just like I was!"

The Rebbetzin would chuckle when she finished telling the story. Then she would beg the patient, "Please do exactly what your doctor orders! And have a *refuah sheleimah!*"

CHAPTER FIFTEEN

Hachnasas Kallah

Many girls visited the Rebbetzin when they became old enough to get married. They knew she was a wise woman. They wanted her advice.

"How will I know whom to marry?" they would ask.

"Only three things are important," the Rebbetzin would reply. "*Middos tovos* (good character traits), *yiras Shamayim* (fear of Heaven), and being serious about Torah study."

When a girl said she saw all three of these things in a young man, the Rebbetzin would hug her. "*Mazel tov!*" she would exclaim. "You are a *kallah!* I'm so happy for you!"

"What should I do to have a healthy marriage?" a *kallah* would ask.

"The way you can have a healthy marriage and be a 'queen' in your home is to treat your husband like a king. The more love and support you give your husband, the more you will receive back in return!"

It is a big *mitzvah* to make a *kallah* happy at her wedding.

To Make the Kallah Happy

R' Chaim's *talmid* R' Avi Sarussi would sometimes drive the Rebbetzin to weddings in Bnei Brak so that she could run in and say *mazel tov*.

"Whose wedding are we going to?" Avi would ask.

Many times the Rebbetzin didn't know the last name of the *chassan* or *kallah*. She would respond: "The *kallah*, whose name for prayer is Sarah bat Rivkah, who is marrying Shalom ben Esther Leah, came to me before her wedding and invited me. I want to just wish a quick *mazel tov* to make the *kallah* happy."

CHAPTER SIXTEEN
Making Peace

Aharon HaKohen was the most famous peace-maker. If "Reuven" and "Shimon" had an argument, Aharon HaKohen worked hard to get them to make up.

"Reuven," he would say. "Shimon is so sorry about what happened. He wants to make peace with you."

Then he would go to Shimon. "Reuven feels terrible about what happened. He wants to make up."

When Reuven and Shimon next met each other, both would begin to cry. "I'm so sorry for what I did!" each would say. "Let's be friends again!"

Aharon HaKohen would smile and thank Hashem that he was able to make peace between the two men.

Like Aharon HaKohen, Rebbetzin Kanievsky felt terrible when she heard that people were not getting along.

A Clean Slate One year, a teacher came to the Rebbetzin's house two hours before Rosh Hashanah. Her eyes were puffy from crying.

"What happened?" asked the worried Rebbetzin.

The teacher explained. "I had a disagreement with the principal of my school. Today, I went to her and apologized. I begged her to forgive me, but she refused. Tonight is Rosh Hashanah. I'm so afraid that I won't have a good year if she does not forgive me before Rosh Hashanah!"

The Rebbetzin saw how upset the young woman was. She borrowed her assistant's cell phone and called the principal, whom she knew personally.

"Hello, how are you?" the Rebbetzin began. "I would like to wish you and your family a *shanah tovah*!

"I am so happy to hear how well your school is being run. You are getting such *zechuyos* for all your hard work teaching Torah and *middos* to Jewish girls."

Only then did the Rebbetzin mention the teacher and the argument.

The principal did not want to forgive the other woman!

The Rebbetzin tried again. "You know how important it is to go into Rosh Hashanah with a 'clean slate'! Hashem will be so proud of you if you put aside your angry feelings and forgive this teacher!"

Finally, the principal agreed, and peace was made between the two women. The Rebbetzin wished them both a *shanah tovah* and hurried back into her kitchen. She still needed to finish preparing for Yom Tov!

What the Rebbetzin had convinced the principal to do was to be "*mevater*" — to give in. This was something the Rebbetzin herself did very well. She never insisted that she was right, or that things had to

The Importance of Being Mevater

go her way. She was very careful not to hurt anyone's feelings. If she thought there was even a tiny chance that she offended someone, she apologized over and over again. Sometimes the other person had no idea what the Rebbetzin was apologizing for!

Through her actions and her stories, she showed that by "giving in," people can earn a reward in *Olam Haba* and even in *Olam Hazeh*.

She often told this next story about how being *mevater* led to a reward in this world.

> The Rebbetzin's father, R' Elyashiv, had to be hospitalized right before Shabbos. A group of his grandchildren and a man who knew all the doctors in the hospital stayed with him over Shabbos. The grandchildren arranged to have a minyan with a Sefer Torah in R' Elyashiv's room, but they didn't have someone to read the Torah.
>
> Shabbos morning, one of the grandchildren was walking through the hall. He saw 16-year-old "Tuviah Schwartz" standing outside his mother's hospital room.
>
> "Are you a baal korei?" R' Elyashiv's grandson asked hopefully.
>
> "I can lein this week's parashah," Tuviah responded.
>
> "Could you be the baal korei for R' Elyashiv?"
>
> "Absolutely!" replied the bachur. He ran to call his father out of his mother's hospital room for Shacharis. They went to R' Elyashiv's room, and Tuviah leined beautifully. R' Elyashiv thanked him.
>
> Then "Mr. Schwartz" approached R' Elyashiv. He said, "Three years ago was Tuviah's bar mitzvah Shabbos. I had told the gabbai that Tuviah would be leining in shul and the gabbai agreed.
>
> "Three days before the bar mitzvah,

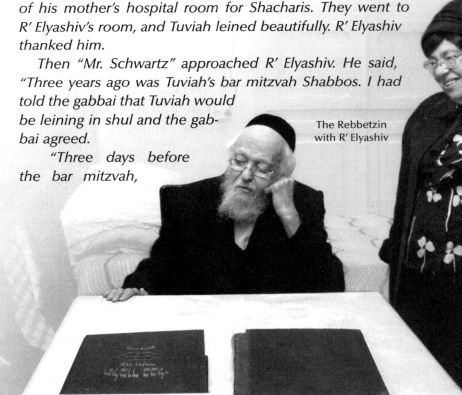

The Rebbetzin with R' Elyashiv

the gabbai called and told us that he had a big problem. He had gotten confused and agreed to let another bar mitzvah boy lein that same week. The gabbai did not know what to do. Which bachur should read the parashah?

"My son thought about this. He had worked very hard to prepare the parashah. But he decided to offer the honor of leining to the other boy.

"Maybe because my son was 'mevater' at his bar mitzvah, he had the honor of reading the Torah for the Rav today," the father said as he finished the story.

R' Elyashiv smiled. "What brings you to the hospital?" he asked.

"My wife has been here for six weeks, but the doctors can't figure out what's wrong with her," Mr. Schwartz replied sadly.

The man who was with R' Elyashiv spoke up. "The famous 'Dr. Gruen' is coming to visit R' Elyashiv tomorrow," he said. "I know him well and will ask him to review Mrs. Schwartz's medical chart."

The next day the specialist came by. After checking R' Elyashiv, he examined Tuviah's mother and said that she had a rare disease. He gave her medicine, and it started to work right away. A few days later, a grateful Mrs. Schwartz was sent home.

Whenever the Rebbetzin told this story, she said: "Tuviah didn't *lein* on the Shabbos of his *bar mitzvah,* but Hashem paid him back for being *mevater.* He had the honor to *lein* for R' Elyashiv, and this helped cure his mother!"

The passport photo of the young Yosef Shalom Elyashiv

CHAPTER SEVENTEEN
Kabbalas Kahal

The Rebbetzin had certain times for visitors to come to her house. This was called her "*kabbalas kahal.*"

Why did people come from all over the world to visit the Rebbetzin? They knew that she truly loved everyone. When she spoke to someone, she tuned out everything else and gave her full attention to the person in front of her. Even if there was a long line of people waiting to see her, and lots of noise, she would only concentrate on one person at a time.

Nothing was allowed to interfere with the Rebbetzin's *kabbalas kahal.* She met with her visitors even when she felt tired or sick, even

The Importance of Kabbalas Kahal when she really needed to rest or take a vacation.

There were times that her family tried to make her rest and not see so many visitors

each day. She insisted that they allow everyone in to see her. If there were not a lot of visitors, she would peek through the window to make sure that nobody was telling visitors not to come up.

Children sometimes came to Rebbetzin Kanievsky for advice. The Rebbetzin would spend time listening to their problems and trying to help them.

Teaching and Learning from Children

The single most important thing that she told children was to be nice to their classmates and not to form cliques which leave out other children.

"If you are making a small party in your house, and some of your classmates will feel bad because they weren't invited, it is better not to make the party in the first place," the Rebbetzin would tell young girls.

"Tzivi" visited the Rebbetzin for the first time when she was 11 years old.

I'm Sure She Would Have Done the Same!

"I'm so sad!" she sobbed. "My marks are terrible, and nobody likes me. I have no friends in school! I stay home by myself after school, in my own room. My parents are always telling me to find something to do, and we end up arguing."

The Rebbetzin hugged Tzivi as she cried. "Which school do you attend?" the Rebbetzin asked softly. When she heard the answer, she said, "My granddaughter Racheli is in the same school, in the same grade, in one of the other classes. She probably does not know what a hard time you are having! May I talk to her about your problems?"

"Okay," mumbled Tzivi.

The Rebbetzin told Racheli about Tzivi's problems. Racheli offered to tutor her so that her marks would get better. She also made sure that other girls became her friends. Soon Tzivi's test scores improved, girls invited her over to play, and she felt better about herself. She also stopped fighting with her parents.

The Rebbetzin was interested in Tzivi's progress. Every week, Racheli told her what was going on.

A few months later, Tzivi visited the Rebbetzin again.

"Thank you for all you have done!" she said. "Everything is so much better now. I'm doing well in school and I have friends. At home, instead of hiding in my room, I help my mother!"

The Rebbetzin smiled and answered, "I didn't help at all. All I did was ask Racheli what was happening. She did the rest. If you would have told Racheli yourself, I'm sure she would have done the same!"

"Daniel" was a 7-year-old boy who was ill. He needed special medical treatments to cure his disease. He asked the Rebbetzin for a special

Not My Peyos!

berachah.

"I know that my hair might fall out because of the treatment, and I'll look different from all the other children," he said. "That's okay. But could you give me a *berachah* that my *peyos* won't fall out?"

The Rebbetzin began to cry when she heard the child's innocent request.

"Please wait here while I discuss this with R' Chaim," she said, and ran out of the room to go speak to her husband.

R' Chaim had a beautiful idea. "I am planning to make a *siyum* tomorrow," he said. "I will dedicate it to Daniel's recovery."

The next day, when Daniel and his father arrived, R' Chaim held the child's hand. He gently asked, "Are you the little *tzaddik* the *Rabbanit* told me about?"

At the end of the *siyum*, R' Chaim drank some wine as he did at every *siyum*. He then offered Daniel a small sip of the *siyum* wine as well.

With Hashem's help, after two more treatments the boy got better. His *peyos* and hair did not fall out.

Some people thought R' Chaim's *siyum* wine had special powers, and started asking for some. "No," said R' Chaim. "It is good to take part in a *siyum*, but there is nothing special about the wine itself."

R' Chaim at a son's *bar mitzvah*

Twelve-year-old "Roni Stern" and his parents came to speak to the Rebbetzin. It was obvious that the young boy was sad. Soon he admit-

Bar Mitzvah Advice ted why. The hall his parents wanted to book for his *bar mitzvah* was not the same one his classmates used for their celebrations. Not only that, but his parents were planning a much plainer party than the other boys had.

"Of course we want our son to be happy," said Mrs. Stern softly.

"But we simply don't have the money to make the fancy *bar mitzvah* that Roni would like," added Mr. Stern.

The Rebbetzin turned to Roni. "I understand that you don't want to feel different from your classmates," she said, "but let me tell you about the *bar mitzvah* of my husband, R' Chaim.

"When R' Chaim became *bar mitzvah*, his father, the Steipler, was a *maggid shiur* in the Novardok Yeshivah in Bnei Brak. The night of his *bar mitzvah*, young Chaim went with his father to the yeshivah for *Maariv*. The Steipler brought along several cakes that his wife had baked, and two bottles of wine.

"After *Maariv*, the Steipler went to the yeshivah dining room. Several of R' Chaim's friends and *rebbeim* joined them. R' Chaim then delivered a *bar mitzvah* speech that he had prepared. Everyone said *mazel tov*, and they danced for a few minutes in the dining room.

"No one had the money to host a meal in those days. They could not even provide challos so that people could wash and *bentch*." The Rebbetzin smiled. "But my husband was happy with his *bar mitzvah* and never complained about it.

"Roni, your parents are trying to make you the nicest *bar mitzvah* possible, while not spending more than they can afford. The most important thing is that you should be happy and use the important occasion of your *bar mitzvah* to get close to Hashem with *simchah*."

R' Chaim's grandson once asked him whether he had received any *bar mitzvah* gifts. "Oh, yes," replied R' Chaim. "I received exactly seven *sefarim* from seven different people. I still have the *sefarim* today. I didn't receive money or any other gifts besides those seven *sefarim*."

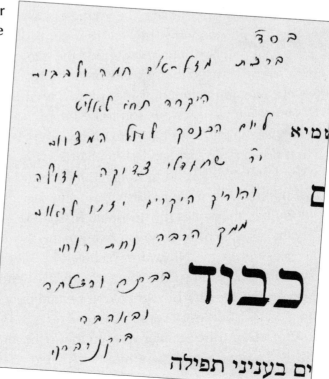

The Rebbetzin's inscription in a *sefer* she presented to each of a group of cousins who had come for a *berachah* before their *bas mitzvah*

Hundreds of young girls from all over the world visited the Rebbetzin before their *bas mitzvah*. She made a special point of showering

Bas Mitzvah Girls

them with attention and giving them a personal gift — a *sefer*, called *Orchos Yosher*, which was written by R' Chaim. This *sefer* discusses how to improve *middos*. On the first page, the Rebbetzin would write warm words of blessing to the *bas mitzvah* girl.

One night the Rebbetzin was in terrible pain. Her doctor said that she must stay in bed that evening to rest. Her daughter Brachah Braverman came to help out in the house because the Rebbetzin was so weak.

Late at night there was a knock on the door. It was a *bas mitzvah* girl who had come to speak to the Rebbetzin and receive an inscribed *sefer* as a gift.

"Brachah!" the Rebbetzin called out. "Please bring my guest into my room."

She sat up in bed as the youngster was ushered in, and spent about 10 minutes with the girl.

After the child left, Brachah asked her mother, "The doctor wanted you to rest. Why didn't you ask the girl to come back tomorrow?"

"I really didn't do anything against the

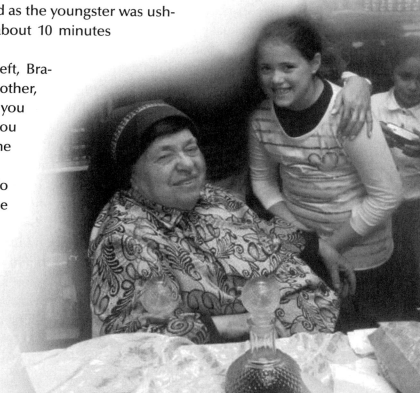

The Rebbetzin with
a visitor just days
before her *petirah*

doctor's orders," replied the Rebbetzin. "I stayed in bed the whole time, even when I inscribed the *sefer*. Even though I was weak and felt sick, how could I disappoint a girl who came to my house?

"From the time of her *bas mitzvah*, a young lady is obligated to keep *mitzvos*," concluded the Rebbetzin. "I have to set a positive example for the girls, even if it is physically difficult for me."

Eleven-year-old Moshe S. was a bright boy who made trouble in class. After the principal suspended him, Moshe's mother brought him to Rebbetzin Kanievsky for a *berachah*.

Daven for Your Classmates

The Rebbetzin gave Moshe some candy. "Why are you not in *cheder* today?" she asked gently.

The boy looked embarrassed. "I was suspended for disturbing the class," he mumbled.

"Why do you disturb the class?" asked the Rebbetzin.

"I'm so bored! Rebbi repeats everything until everyone understands it. I usually understand the first time!" he said proudly.

The Rebbetzin smiled. "I understand," she told the boy. "Come here and sit in the Steipler's chair. I would like you to say *Tehillim* for the next 20 minutes. *Daven* that your classmates should understand the *rebbi*'s lessons more quickly. Then the class can move on to the next lesson and you won't be bored."

About 20 minutes later, the Rebbetzin said, "Moshe, I've been watching you *daven* on the Steipler's chair. I am very impressed with your sincerity. Someday you will grow up to be a *tzaddik*!"

She then inscribed a *sefer Tehillim* and gave it to him. She then told the boy, "From now on I want you to bring this *Tehillim* with you every day to school. If your classmates don't understand the lesson as quickly as you do, please take out your *Tehillim* in class and *daven* that your classmates should understand the lesson faster."

From that time on, whenever Moshe was bored in class, he used the time to *daven* for his classmates to understand faster.

The Rebbetzin loved and respected teachers. "You are so lucky to be teaching Torah to *bnos Yisrael*!" she would tell them sincerely. She

Who Needs a Torah Education?

advised people to *daven* for their children to be righteous. She also told people — even if they were not yet religious — to send their children to yeshivah.

"Why should I send my children to yeshivah?" people would ask the Rebbetzin. "Why can't I send them to public school?"

"Let me tell you a story about my granddaughter Chana," the Rebbetzin would answer.

> "One day, 5-year-old Chana was with me when an ambulance stopped in front of a neighbor's house. Right away, Chana began saying Tehillim by heart.
>
> "I was so surprised. 'Chana, where did you learn to say Tehillim?' I asked her.
>
> "She replied in her childish little voice, 'In kindergarten, Morah taught us that if we see an ambulance, we should daven. The person inside the ambulance may need our tefillos. Morah taught us a few chapters of Tehillim. That's what I just said.'"

The Steipler with
Yitzchak Shaul (Shuki),
then age 9

"Wow!" people would answer. "Is that what they teach the children in yeshivah? To care about other people!"

"I have another story to tell you about Chana," the Rebbetzin would respond.

"Chana came to visit me, and she was very sad.

"'What happened to make you so unhappy?' I asked.

"'Today, in kindergarten, Rivka told me that Devorah's savta died last week.'

"'That really is very sad,' I agreed. 'Did you speak to Devorah about it?'

"'Oh, no!' replied Chana. 'Maybe Devorah doesn't know yet! I don't want to speak about it. I don't want her to hear about it from me. I don't want to make her sad.'"

"Now do you understand why you should send your children to yeshivah?" the Rebbetzin would ask. "Such kind behavior comes only when children learn Torah and middos tovos!"

Sometimes you really, really want something, but if you get it, someone else might get hurt. What should you do?

The Kindness of Children

Many people asked the Rebbetzin questions like this. Instead of an answer, she sometimes told this story about her granddaughters.

Rutie and Yehudit were 7 years old. They were cousins and best friends, and they were in the same class at school. They loved to come together to visit their savta.

"Savta," said Rutie one day, at the end of the school year, "this year we did not sit next to each other in class, but we decided that next year we will sit together."

The Rebbetzin was very happy that her granddaughters were so close. "That is an excellent idea!" she said, and hugged them both.

At the beginning of the new school year, the Rebbetzin asked, "So, Rutie, do you enjoy sitting next to Yehudit?"

Rutie looked down and said, "Savta, you know how badly I wanted to sit next to Yehudit. But on the first day of school, Rivkah Cohen asked me to sit next to her. I didn't want to make Rivkah feel bad, so I sat next to her instead of sitting next to Yehudit."

The Rebbetzin was very proud of Rutie for being careful with other people's feelings

---

Partners

Seminary Girls

For many years, girls from high schools and seminaries came in groups to visit Rebbetzin Kanievsky. They asked for *berachos*, and then the Rebbetzin posed for pictures with each girl.

The Rebbetzin told them: "When you get married, if you allow your husband to dedicate himself to Torah study, you will be an equal partner when it comes to getting a reward. You will sit next to him in Gan Eden, and understand the Torah he has learned.

"If there is a man who is great in Torah learning, there is a great woman behind him. If a man's wife takes care of the children, serves him his meals, and takes care of day-to-day matters, he will have much more time to learn."

A *kallah* came to the Rebbetzin for a *berachah* on her wedding day.

Advice for a Kallah

"Please give me a *berachah* that my husband should be a *tzaddik* like R' Chaim," she begged.

"I will give you a *berachah* that your husband should be a big *talmid chacham*. But he cannot do it alone. You will have to help him if you want him to learn a lot.

"For the first few years after we got married, I hardly visited my family in Yerushalayim. I really missed them all, especially my baby sister Gitta! When I saw other young couples going to Yerushalayim for Shabbos or Yom Tov, I used to cry, because it made me think of going to Yerushalayim to visit my family. But I knew that it was very important for my husband to be near his father, the Steipler, and near the Chazon Ish. I was prepared to sacrifice, even though it was very hard. I was willing and happy to do it.

"If you and your future husband will dedicate yourselves completely to Torah, he can be a *gadol b'Yisrael. Mazel tov!*"

—————— Supporting Torah ——————

The Rebbetzin always told people how important it is to support someone who is learning. There are many ways to show support, and she had stories and advice about them all.

This story that she heard from R' Chaim was one of her favorites. There was a young Torah scholar who lived in a small town in Rus-

A Missed Opportunity sia. He learned diligently every day in the shul.

"You are so thin!" said his friend. "You are learning all day long, and you probably don't have enough money for food. Come work in my lumberyard and earn some money!"

"No, thank you," replied the Torah scholar. "I want to learn full time and become a *rav.*"

His friend got very angry. When they met in shul, he would jingle coins in the scholar's face and tease him. "Don't be so lazy! Stop wasting your time learning! You could make a lot of money if you went to work. I see how poor you are!"

The young scholar, R' Yitzchak Elchanan Spector, continued to learn, and became the Rav of Kovno. He was one of the greatest *rabbanim* in the world.

One day his friend visited him.

"I'm so impressed!" he said. "You are a famous *rav*! I would like to help support you."

"No, thank you," said R' Yitzchak Elchanan politely. "Many years ago, when I was young and poor and no one had heard of me, you had the chance to help me. You would have had a tremendous *mitzvah* for supporting a struggling scholar. But you lost your chance to have this *zechus*."

"Chavi" was earning a good *parnassah* and was saving a lot of money. But she was not so young anymore, and she was still not mar-ried.

Torah Is the Best Segulah!

"What can I do to help find my *basherte*?" she asked the Rebbetzin.

The Rebbetzin replied, "My husband says it is good to give your *maaser* to a *kollel* because Torah is the best *segulah*."

"Actually," Chavi said, "I must have enough *maaser* money saved up by now to pay for a whole *kollel*!"

Chavi gave her money to open a brand new *kollel*. Exactly one year later, she got engaged!

The Rebbetzin lived her entire life in Eretz Yisrael, and never traveled to *chutz la'aretz*. She rarely left her humble home on Rechov Rashbam. She did not have a telephone, and she hardly read the newspaper. But she understood exactly what was going on in the world.

Sitting and Talking

Sometimes women or girls came just to meet the Rebbetzin and ask for a *berachah*. They had nothing special that they wanted to discuss. She would beg them to get rid of Internet access in their homes or on their phones. She would talk to them about Shabbos and *tznius*. She explained how important it was not to talk *lashon hara* or embarrass others. Of course, she always had wonderful stories to tell.

The Rebbetzin was very careful about other people's feelings. She never wanted to hurt anyone.

One hot day, she was sitting with a group of women in her house.

"It's a little warm in here," she commented. "I'm getting a little thirsty."

Twelve women jumped up and ran to the kitchen to bring the Rebbetzin a glass of water!

Now what should she do? How could she avoid hurting anyone's feelings? You guessed it: she drank a little water from every single glass. She must have been really thirsty — for *mitzvos*

Shabbos

R' Chaim told the Rebbetzin that if a non-religious person asks which single *mitzvah* s/he should try to keep, the answer should be *shemiras Shabbos*.

"Shuly's" 14-year-old daughter was very sick. Shuly came to the Rebbetzin and asked for a *berachah* that her child should have a *refuah sheleimah*.

"Do you keep Shabbos?" the Rebbetzin asked.

"No," Shuly admitted.

The Rebbetzin explained that Shabbos is the source of *berachah* and that keeping Shabbos will let the *berachos* flow. Shuly promised to consider the Rebbetzin's words. Then she went straight to the hospital.

When she arrived, her daughter said, "Ima, I've been thinking what I could do as a *zechus* to help me get better. I decided to observe Shabbos."

Both Shuly and her daughter started to keep Shabbos. After a while, with Hashem's help, the girl was completely healed.

The Rebbetzin always dressed very modestly. In fact, this was the first thing her future mother-in-law noticed the first time they met. It **Tznius** helped her decide that Batsheva Elyashiv would be a good wife for her dear son, R' Chaim.

"If a girl dresses with *tznius*, it can prevent bad things from happening to Jews around the world," the Rebbetzin would say. A lack of *tznius* bothered her more than anything else.

"Hila" was a lady from Tel Aviv who loved clothes. She had a huge wardrobe of clothing in the latest styles. Her friends all admired her **Hila's Sacrifice** outfits and thought she was very well dressed. But her clothes were not modest.

One day Hila's doctor told her that she was very sick and might not live much longer.

Hila visited the Rebbetzin to discuss her illness. "What can I do as a *zechus* for a *refuah sheleimah*?" she asked.

"If you start dressing modestly, the change in the way you look will be noticed by your friends — and in *Shamayim*," answered the Rebbetzin.

A letter to seminary girls:
"Each girl should accept on herself to daven with concentration and to study two halachos regarding proper speech, because this prevents many tragedies and brings much salvation, and obviously to be very careful that one should be dressed with tznius ...."

Hila's next doctor's visit was not encouraging. He did not think she would get better.

Hila decided to become a *baalas teshuvah*. She went home and threw all her immodest clothing into a dark garbage bag and dumped it. She also began keeping Shabbos.

After keeping Shabbos for a few weeks, she had an operation. Eventually she had a full recovery.

The Rebbetzin said that it was Hila's sacrifice that cured her. She gave up what was most precious to her: her collection of clothing. Hashem saw this, and healed her from her illness.

Today, Hila and her family are all religious.

One of the Rebbetzin's favorite *tznius* stories starred her little granddaughter.

The Missing Button

"Zev" and his two teenaged children were starting to become *frum*. Only Zev's wife, "Hadar," did not want to change the way they lived. One day the family was in Bnei Brak, and Zev and the children went to speak to the Rebbetzin. Hadar wasn't interested and waited outside the room.

All of sudden, the Rebbetzin's 6-year-old granddaughter showed up, sobbing. Hadar brought the child to the Rebbetzin. "Your granddaughter seems very upset," she said.

The Rebbetzin hugged the little girl. "Why are you crying?" she asked.

"I'm sure Hashem is mad at me," the little girl hiccuped through her tears, "and I need your help. The top button of my blouse ripped off and I'm not *tzniusdik* now. Savta, do you think Hashem will be mad at me? Do you think I could do *teshuvah*? It was an accident that the button fell off! I will do my best to make sure that it doesn't happen again!"

When Hadar heard this, she burst out crying. "If such a young girl can be on such a high level," she declared, "I will try to begin keeping *mitzvos*, too."

Sometimes the Rebbetzin's words went straight into a woman's heart and the woman would want to change right away. More than once, the Rebbetzin gave a pair of her own tights to someone who came in without stockings and, after speaking to the Rebbetzin, was embarrassed to leave her house the same way!

Miracle in the Mall

Before Pesach of 2009, a group of 40 young women from a seminary in Tzefas visited the Rebbetzin. The girls were not modestly dressed, but the Rebbetzin believed they were trying to grow in *mitzvah* observance. After telling them stories about *tznius*, she suggested, "Why don't you all go shopping together to buy a modest outfit for each one of you?"

The next week, on Motza'ei Shabbos, March 21, the 40 young women boarded the same bus that had taken them to Rebbetzin Kanievsky in Bnei Brak. But this time they went to the Lev HaMifratz mall in Haifa.

While they were shopping for *tzniusdik* clothing at the mall, a miracle happened. Arab terrorists had parked a white car containing explosives in the mall. With Hashem's help, the bomb didn't go off. People saw smoke coming out of the car and called the police.

The prime minister of Israel declared: "A huge disaster was avoided" because this huge explosive failed. Had the bomb detonated, the entire Lev HaMifratz mall would have been in danger of collapsing.

The plastic bag containing the remains of the clothing a girl shredded after the miracle at the Lev HaMifratz mall

The prime minister wasn't sure why the bomb had failed. However, the Rebbetzin and the seminary students from Tzefas were sure they knew the answer. It was because 40 girls had decided to dress in a more modest way and were shopping for clothing in that very mall at exactly the time the bomb was supposed to go off!

In their new, *tzniusdik* clothes, the girls returned to the Rebbetzin's house two days later to celebrate the miracle. They informed her that they had thrown out their immodest clothing. One of the girls had shredded a non-*tzniusdik* outfit, and she gave it to the Rebbetzin as a gift in a small plastic bag.

An elderly woman from Yerushalayim was waiting to see the Rebbetzin. Her son, who studied in a *kollel* in Yerushalayim, was with her. The line was long and moving slowly.

A Wise Solution

The *avreich* approached the Rebbetzin. "Could my mother possibly go to the front of the line?" he asked. "She needs someone to help her get home, and I need to get back to *kollel* as soon as possible."

What should the Rebbetzin do? She did not want to be responsible for the young man's *bitul Torah*, but it was not fair to allow someone to cut the line.

"How wonderful it is that you have such a love for learning!" she said to the young man. "So, why don't you return to your *kollel* right away? Many people come here from many different neighborhoods.

I'm sure I could ask someone to take your mother home. If I don't find someone, I will take her back myself when the *kabbalas kahal* is over."

This way the Rebbetzin was able to avoid both *bitul Torah* and letting someone unfairly cut the line!

Too Busy to Rest

Dr. Meshulam Hart was concerned about the health of his patient, Rebbetzin Batsheva Kanievsky. She was overtired, and the doctor told her that she needed a vacation. R' Chaim agreed to try to convince her to go, but weeks passed and she was still home.

Finally, Dr. Hart went to Yerushalayim to consult R' Elyashiv. He suggested that Batsheva should come to Yerushalayim and rest in his home. While there, she would have a very limited *kabbalas kahal*.

Dr. Hart returned to Bnei Brak and told the Rebbetzin what her father had said. The next morning, she packed a small suitcase and traveled to her father's home.

That evening, Dr. Hart heard that the Rebbetzin had already returned to Bnei Brak! He could not believe his ears! Dr. Hart headed

R' Chaim with Dr. Hart

straight to 23 Rechov Rashbam. There was the Rebbetzin with a crowd of women around her, having her *kabbalas kahal* as usual.

"Why did you return?" he asked. "What happened in your father's house in Yerushalayim?"

The Rebbetzin had explained to R' Elyashiv that she didn't need a vacation or a rest. She had told her father about the questions people come to discuss with her. R' Elyashiv agreed with her about the importance of her work, and she came back home.

From that day on, the Rebbetzin never took a vacation or spent even one day away from home to rest.

One time when she wasn't feeling well, her doctor was called in. He said that she looked very tired. R' Chaim said he would make sure that she rested.

When the doctor arrived the next day, he found R' Chaim sitting by the front door and learning. He was blocking anyone from entering the house. The doctor was very pleased when he saw that the Rebbetzin was resting in bed.

The next day the room was crowded as always. The doctor quickly found R' Chaim. "What happened with the Rebbetzin's resting?" he asked. "Perhaps the Rav wasn't a good guard?"

R' Chaim replied that it was doing his wife more harm than good to stay in bed and not receive her visitors. The doctor and R' Chaim finally agreed that it would be better for her health to continue seeing her visitors.

R' Chaim's Kabbalas Kahal

Every day, R' Chaim learns, writes his *sefarim*, and answers letters. Then he has a *kabbalas kahal* for men. He wishes them "*berachah v'hatzlachah.*" He remembers the names of all the people who ask for his *tefillos* and *berachos,* and *davens* for them.

One night, the people who usually helped out during R' Chaim's *kabbalas kahal* could not come. R' Chaim decided not to receive

R' Meir Zlotowitz (r) gives R' Chaim one of the first volumes of the Hebrew Edition of ArtScroll's Schottenstein Talmud. R' Shlomo Kanievsky is standing in the center.

any visitors that night. Instead, he spent his usual *kabbalas kahal* time learning upstairs. He enjoyed learning without interruption.

When R' Chaim later went to bed for his regular 2½ hours of rest, he could not fall asleep. The next day, he thought he understood why. *Yidden* had come to discuss their problems with him, and he wasn't available. Hashem punished him by not allowing him to sleep, because he should have tried harder to get someone to assist him!

The Rebbetzin's husband (R' Chaim Kanievsky), her father (R' Elyashiv), and her father-in-law (the Steipler Gaon) all agreed that Batsheva

Whose Berachos Are Stronger?

Kanievsky had a special power of *tefillah*. Because of her *savlanus* (patience), her love for all Jews, and her *chessed*, they were sure that Hashem heard her prayers. In fact, R' Chaim used to ask the Rebbetzin to give him *berachos* before Yom Kippur and at other times of the year.

The Rebbetzin was asked many times, "Whose *berachos* or *tefillos* are more readily accepted by Hashem — yours or R' Chaim's?" She usually answered that R' Chaim's *berachos* were more effective than hers. Then she would tell the following story:

A man was waiting on line to get a *berachah* from R' Chaim. When he saw the Rebbetzin, he began to cry. "Please *daven* for me and my wife!" he begged. "We are married for many years and we still don't have children!"

The Rebbetzin encouraged him. "May Hashem bless you with healthy twins!" was her sincere *berachah*.

A few minutes later, the man entered R' Chaim's room and asked him for a *berachah*. "The Rebbetzin already gave me a *berachah* that we should have twins!" he informed R' Chaim.

R' Chaim smiled and said, "Only twins? I give you a *berachah* that you should have triplets!" Sure enough, the couple was blessed with healthy triplets!

"That is proof," said the Rebbetzin, "that R' Chaim's *berachos* are better than mine!"

Both R' Chaim and the Rebbetzin *davened* hard for the people who came to them for help. Unfortunately, some people only came to

Sharing Good News share their problems, but forgot to come back when their problem was solved. The Rebbetzin begged her visitors to come back and share good news. When they did, the Rebbetzin would smile from ear to ear. The Kanievskys considered this their reward for *davening*.

A young man asked R' Chaim for a *berachah* to have more children. "We have been married for 12 years," he said, "and we have only

Four Years Late one daughter, who is 4 years old."

"When was your daughter born?" R' Chaim asked.

"Four years ago," replied the man.

R' Chaim again asked the young man, "When was your daughter born?"

"Four years ago," he responded once more.

R' Chaim and the Rebbetzin serving as *kvatter* at the *bris* of a great-grandchild, born to their grandchild after several years of marriage

R' Chaim then gave him a *berachah* that he should have more children.

Later, R' Chaim told his son-in-law, "Some people come and ask for *berachos* but never return to share the good news. I did not recognize the face of the young man who asked me for a *berachah* for more children. But when he gave me his name and his wife's, I immediately remembered their names from eight years ago. I have had them in mind in my *davening* every day for the last eight years. I wish they would have come four years ago and shared the good news that they had a daughter!"

"Mrs. Greenberg" often *davened* in the Lederman Shul on Friday nights. During the years before the Greenbergs were blessed with children, Rebbetzin Kanievsky would encourage her neighbor and give her *berachos*.

Where Is His Twin?

When Mrs. Greenberg was finally blessed with twin boys, the Rebbetzin was so happy and excited! She rushed to visit the new mother in the hospital to wish her *mazel tov*.

Mrs. Greenberg would bring the boys to the Lederman Shul every Friday night to wish the Rebbetzin a good Shabbos. One Shabbos, when the twins were 3 years old, Mrs. Greenberg came by with only "Muttie." His twin brother, "Itzik," was playing with some boys in the neighborhood.

"Where is Itzik?" the Rebbetzin asked. "It makes my Shabbos so special when I see your twins together every Friday night."

Not wanting to disappoint the Rebbetzin, Mrs. Greenberg went down the block and returned with both sons. A huge smile spread across the Rebbetzin's face as she hugged and kissed the little boys. "This is true happiness on Shabbos!" she cried.

The Rebbetzin passed away the next afternoon after *Minchah*. Until the very end of her life, she shared the happiness of others with her whole heart.

CHAPTER EIGHTEEN

The Power of Learning

Why did the Rebbetzin's father (R' Elyashiv) and her husband (R' Chaim) become such big *talmidei chachamim*?

The Rebbetzin said it was because of their *hasmadah*. (They spent a lot of time learning Torah.) "You don't have to be born smart to become a big *talmid chacham* (or get really good marks in school). But you do have to work hard and have *yiras Shamayim*."

When R' Chaim was learning, he was hardly aware of what was going on around him. All he could think about was Torah. He did not

A Model of Hasmadah

notice the Rebbetzin if she came into the *cheder hasefarim* to ask a question. Even if she motioned with her hands, he did not see her. He only realized she was there after she called his name a few times.

Sometimes people approached the Rebbetzin while R' Chaim was busy learning, answering letters, or writing his *sefarim*. They begged her to let them in to see R' Chaim. It was not time for his *kabbalas kahal*, and he did not wish to be interrupted, so she asked them to come back later. If they preferred to wait, she invited them to look through a window and watch R' Chaim learn.

"Spend as much time as you wish. Don't worry about standing there," she would say. "R' Chaim is so absorbed in his studies that he never notices anyone at the window. You can watch him learning for as long as you like."

A neighbor was planning to have some construction work done in his house. "We will have to drill for two days," the neighbor said.

Not While He Sleeps!

"What time should we drill? When would it bother you the least?"

The Rebbetzin said, "You can drill while R' Chaim is learning."

"While he is learning?" asked the neighbor, surprised. "But won't the noise disturb him?"

"Oh, no!" smiled the Rebbetzin. "He doesn't hear anything when he is busy learning. But please don't drill during his nap time. That would disturb his sleep!"

During the Persian Gulf War of 1991, Saddam Hussein, the leader of Iraq, threatened to shoot rockets into the area of Eretz Yisrael where

Protected by Torah Learning

Tel Aviv and Bnei Brak are located. Many citizens ran away to other countries or to other parts of Eretz Yisrael.

Frightened men and women asked R' Chaim and the Rebbetzin: "Should we stay here in Bnei Brak, or should we go to Yerushalayim?"

"No harm will come to Bnei Brak!" declared R' Chaim. He told all those who asked his opinion to stay in Bnei Brak and not leave.

When the women asked the Rebbetzin's advice, she told them, "My husband says there is nothing to worry about. Tens of thousands of pages of *Gemara* are protecting Bnei Brak. Tell your husbands to learn more pages of *Gemara* to strengthen Bnei Brak's supershield!"

After R' Shmuel Grossbard was *niftar*, R' Chaim visited the family to fulfill the *mitzvah* of *nichum aveilim*.

R' Chaim's Army Career

After sitting down, R' Chaim said, "I have *hakaras hatov* for your father, *z"l*, who was my commander in the army and helped me a lot!"

Everyone was surprised. Had R' Chaim really been in the army?

"We never heard this before about our father — or about the Rav!" replied one of the mourners.

R' Chaim told them the story.

"It was during the War of Independence, when we were learning in the Lomza Yeshivah in Petach Tikva. The war started, and everyone was drafted into the army. We knew nothing in advance. One day, a large bus pulled up outside the yeshivah. We were told that everybody had to get in and go protect the country.

"None of us even knew how to hold a gun. They gave us sticks and stones and sent us to guard a large hill. Everyone was very scared. One boy hid in a bathroom in the yeshivah and avoided joining the army. But I went with the other *bachurim*, together with my roommate, Moshe. He was sitting beside me the whole time, saying *Tehillim* and crying.

"Your father, R' Grossbard, was the oldest in the group. He was appointed commander and he got the largest stick.

"When we reached the hill, I asked him what we should do. He told me, 'You should go up the hill and sit and learn where they can't see you. Take a stick and two stones so if any Arabs come, you can scare them away.'

"We sat there for a long time. After we left the place, we were told that some Arabs shot live gunfire near the place we stood. We were learning; we did not notice."

When he finished telling this story, R' Chaim said, "Out of gratitude for what your father did then, I am now coming to be *menachem avel.*"

After the State of Israel was founded, all young men had to appear before the Lishkat Hagiyus (Conscription Office). *Bachurim* who were fit to serve in the army were given the chance to continue their Torah studies and put off going into the army, based on the agreement worked out between R' Yitzchak Meir Levin and Israel's first prime minister, David Ben-Gurion. Those who were not healthy enough for army service were given a permanent exemption.

It was R' Chaim's turn to be interviewed.

"Which yeshivah do you attend?" asked the screener.

"Lomza Yeshivah in Petach Tikva," R' Chaim answered.

"On which street is this yeshivah located?"

R' Chaim said that he wasn't sure of the address or the name of the street.

"Do you know which street it is near?"

He replied that he wasn't sure about any of the street names. "But I know how to get there from Bnei Brak by bus!" he said.

"Oh, come on! You've been in the yeshivah for years! You must know the name of the street it is on!"

Over and over again, R' Chaim sincerely replied that he had no idea.

After several more questions and answers, R' Chaim was given a permanent exemption from the army. Since he was not aware of his surroundings, they decided, he would not make a very good soldier!

R' Yonason Strasser and his wife, Freeda, give a lot of money to a *kollel* in Eretz Yisrael that is run by the Rebbetzin's brother, R' Binyamin Elyashiv. R' Binyamin is the author of many vol-

The Greatest Joy

umes on the Talmud, called *Yad Binyamin*.

During a visit from America, the Strassers wished to meet the Rebbetzin. R' Binyamin offered to take them to his sister's home.

After the visit, Rebbetzin Kanievsky turned to the Strassers. "I must thank you!" she said. "I have not seen my brother Binyamin for more than five years!"

R' Yonasan and his wife were very surprised. "Don't you meet at family *s'machos*?" they asked.

"No," answered the Rebbetzin. "At a *simchah*, I always stay in the ladies' section and Binyamin stays with the men."

"Then why don't you just get together once a year so that you can see your brother?" asked one of the Strassers.

"*Chas v'shalom!*" cried the Rebbetzin. "Even though I am very happy to see my brother, I am even happier that he is writing more and more volumes of his *Yad Binyamin*!"

At the wedding of R' Binyamin Elyashiv. In the foreground
(l-r) R' Michel Yehudah Lefkowitz, R' Binyamin Elyashiv, R' Aryeh Levin (standing),
R' Betzalel Zolti, R' Yosef Shalom Elyashiv

CHAPTER NINETEEN
More Mitzvos

According to *Halachah,* a *mezuzah* must be checked twice every seven years. When people came to the Rebbetzin with a problem, she advised them to have their *mezuzos* checked to make sure no letters were missing or faded. "And when you put the *mezuzah* back into the case, make sure it is not put in upside down!" she would add.

Checking the Mezuzos

Avraham Yeshayah, the oldest son of R' Chaim and the Rebbetzin, was responsible for checking the Kanievskys' *mezuzos* once every three and a half years. He would take the *mezuzos* down, have them checked the same day, and then put them back.

When he was about 16 years old, he took down the *mezuzos* and replaced them the same day. The next morning, the Rebbetzin didn't feel well. She was hardly able to get out of bed.

"I am sick today with something I did not have yesterday," she told her son. "Could you please make sure that all the *mezuzos* were put back properly into their cases?"

Avraham Yeshayah checked. Sure enough, he found out that the *mezuzah,* in the doorway to his parents' bedroom was not kosher! He had accidentally damaged it when he nailed the case back onto the doorpost.

Avraham Yeshayah immediately went to the *sofer,* bought a new *mezuzah,* and put it up. The Rebbetzin felt better almost immediately.

The Steipler and the Chazon Ish used to go out of their way to be *sandek* at a *bris*. R' Chaim Kanievsky does the same. On one day he was *sandek* eight times in five different cities all over Eretz Yisrael! R' Chaim left his house early that morning and returned home close to 5:00 in the afternoon.

Being a Sandek

Whenever R' Chaim and his driver went out of town for a *bris*, the Rebbetzin prepared two baskets filled with food and drinks. She carefully packed a pot of rice and enough food to feed 10 people! When the driver, R' Shaya, said that the Rebbetzin was sending too much food, she replied, "If you bring me the leftovers, I will eat them!"

The Steipler serving as *sandek*

R' Chaim serving as *sandek*. Notice how he keeps his *tallis* covering the baby's head.

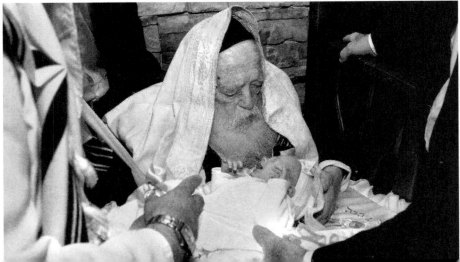

One winter, R' Chaim was going to a *bris* in Yerushalayim to be *sandek*. The day before, there was a snowstorm there. It hardly ever snows in Eretz Yisrael. The Rebbetzin was asked if she would like to go along and see the snow.

"No, thank you. I have to be here for the women who come to see me," she answered. Then she admitted, "Besides, I have bad memories about snowstorms."

"Why? What happened to you in the snow?"

"When I was 17 years old I was working as a bookkeeper, and Yerushalayim was hit with a rare blizzard. My family depended on my salary, so I could not stay home from work. The soles of my shoes had a hole in them, so I borrowed the shoes of my older brother, Shlomo. But his shoes were huge! They filled up with snow as I walked to work. By the time I got there, my feet were frozen! And then the same thing happened when I walked home from work later.

"That's why I have no wish to see a large snowfall again!"

CHAPTER TWENTY
The Rebbetzin's Petirah

The Rebbetzin's life ended suddenly on Shabbos Chol Hamoed Succos (17 Tishrei), 2011. Thousands of women all over the world felt as if they had lost their mother, grandmother, or best friend.

Just a few days earlier, on Motza'ei Yom Tov of the first day of Succos, the Rebbetzin had visited her father, R' Elyashiv, in Yerushalayim. She also visited her brother R' Shlomo in a nursing home, and she and R' Chaim went to the *Kosel*.

The Rebbetzin's last visit to her father

Her Last Hour

The last day of the Rebbetzin's life was filled with *mitzvos* and *chessed*, just like every other day of her life.

The Rebbetzin davened *Minchah* at 12:30 in the Lederman Shul. As she was about to go upstairs, "Chani" approached her. "Please give me a *berachah*!" she begged. "I'm already over 30 years old, and I am still single!" The Rebbetzin gave her a warm *berachah* that she should become a *kallah* very soon. Chani thanked the Rebbetzin for her warm words and turned away. (Within four weeks, Chani was engaged.)

The Rebbetzin shortly before her *petirah*

Then Sarah walked the Rebbetzin up the steps. "Wish me *mazel tov*!" she said. "One of my children had a baby before Succos!"

The Rebbetzin hugged and kissed her. "Sarah," she exclaimed, "thanks for sharing the wonderful news with me! I really miss you since you moved to Tzefas." Sarah discussed a personal issue with the Rebbetzin and received a *berachah*. Then the Rebbetzin entered her house.

The *Tehillim* she was clutching as she passed away

She went into her bedroom and took challos out of the freezer for *seudah shelishis*. Lydia, who visited often, got a *berachah* from the Rebbetzin regarding a personal matter. With Lydia sitting by her side, the Rebbetzin began to say *Tehillim*. It was her custom to complete the entire *sefer Tehillim* every Shabbos.

Two minutes later, with her *sefer Tehillim* held firmly in her hand, and wearing her Shabbos finery, she suffered a heart attack. The Rebbetzin's huge heart, which was filled with *ahavas Yisrael*, had stopped beating.

The family called for help. Dr. Hart, Hatzalah, and Magen David Adom were there within moments.

"Give us a *berachah* that we should be able to save your wife!" begged the medics. R' Chaim looked up from his *Tehillim* and wished them "*Berachah v'hatzlachah*."

Finally, Dr. Hart walked into the room where R' Chaim and Shuki were *davening* for a miracle. With tears streaming down his face, he told R' Chaim that they had done everything possible, but they were unable to restart the Rebbetzin's great heart.

"Did you have a chance to say *Shema Yisrael* with her?" asked R' Chaim.

"Yes," replied Dr. Hart. "The Hatzalah members said *Shema* around her body."

The *levayah* took place that same night. Thousands of people attended. Later, dozens of *hespedim* were given in many cities in Eretz Yisrael and in many other countries. Everyone felt as if they had lost someone very dear to them.

Signs about the *levayah*

R' Chaim and his sons during shivah; l-r: R' Shlomo, R' Yitzchak Shaul, R' Chaim, R' Avraham Yeshayah

R' Chaim leaving his house after *shivah*

Two weeks after the Rebbetzin's *petirah*, a rich man from the United States came to R' Chaim.

In Memory of the Rebbetzin

Flipping open his checkbook, he said, "In memory of the Rebbetzin, I would like to donate money to any *tzedakah* that the Rav will choose."

"What are you learning now?" asked R' Chaim. "How much time do you spend learning every day?" After the man answered, R' Chaim said, "In memory of the Rebbetzin, I would like you to add a half-hour of learning to your day and start learning *Mishnayos Zera'im*."

"I would rather make a very large donation," said the rich man. "To whom should I write a check?"

"I heard you the first time," R' Chaim replied, "but if you really want to do something special for the Rebbetzin's *neshamah*, you should learn an extra half-hour each day and not get off 'easy' by writing a check!"

Thousands of people named their newborn daughters Batsheva Esther after the Rebbetzin. The day after the Rebbetzin passed away, at least three newborn girls in Israel were already given the name Batsheva Esther.

Three months after the Rebbetzin passed away, one of R' Chaim's sons saw his father crying.

Later...

"Abba," he said, "we do our best to help you in every way. Is there anything else that we can do?"

R' Chaim thanked him for all his efforts. "I just miss Ima very much," he admitted.

He is not alone.

Yehi zichrah baruch.

Glossary

All words are Hebrew unless indicated otherwise

ahavas Yisrael – love of Jews

almanah [pl. almanos] – widows

Asher Yatzar – the blessing after one uses the bathroom

aufruf – *(Yiddish)* When the chassan is called up to the Torah on the Shabbos before his wedding

avreich – a married young man, usually one still learning in yeshivah

baal korei – the one who reads aloud from the Torah

baal [male] / baalas [female] teshuvah [pl. baalei / baalos teshuvah] – one who returns to Jewish life and observance

bachur [pl. bachurim] – single young man

basherte – *(Yiddish)* the one a person is supposed to marry

becher – *(Yiddish)* Kiddush cup

bedikas chametz – the search for chametz, done the night before Pesach

beis hamidrash – study hall, place where people learn

berachah [pl. berachos] – blessing. There are berachos before and after eating food, before doing mitzvos, and asking or thanking Hashem for things. People also ask righteous people for berachos, which are good wishes for things they need or want.

Berachah v'hatzlachah – "You should have blessing and success"

bikur cholim – visiting people who are sick

Bircas HaMazon – the blessings after eating a meal with bread

Birchos HaShachar – the blessings we say in the morning, thanking Hashem

Birchos HaTorah – the blessings before learning Torah

bitachon – security; relying on Hashem

bitul Torah – wasting time from learning Torah

bnos Yisrael – Jewish girls

bris [pl. brisos], bris milah – circumcision

challah – special loaves of bread, often braided, for Shabbos, Yom Tov, and other special meals. Also, the piece of dough that must be separated and is burned

chametz – food and products that include grains and that are not allowed on Pesach

Chanukah gelt – *(Yiddish)* money given to children as gifts on Chanukah

chas v'shalom – May Hashem prevent that from happening

chassan [pl. chassanim] – a groom

chavrusa – a study partner

cheder – room; an elementary yeshivah

cheder hasefarim – room where *sefarim* are kept

chessed – kindness

chinuch – training, education

chizuk –encouragement

chovos – debts; here it means the daily learning that R' Chaim and the Rebbetzin undertook to learn

chuppah – wedding canopy; the marriage ceremony

chutz la'aretz – lands outside Eretz Yisrael

Daf Yomi – a program where one two-sided page of Gemara is learned every day

daven – pray

d'mei Chanukah – money given to children as gifts on Chanukah

dvar Torah – a Torah thought

emunah – belief in Hashem

ezras nashim – ladies' section

frum – one who keeps Torah and mitzvos

gabbai – assistant to a rabbi; the person who gives out the honors in shul

gadol, gadol b'Yisrael [pl. gedolim] – a great person, a Torah giant

gashmiyus – physical

gemilus chassadim – doing kind acts

ger [male] / giyores [female] – a convert to Judaism

grushim – small coins

hachnasas kallah – helping someone get married

hachnasas orchim – taking in guests

hadlakas neiros – lighting candles, esp. for Shabbos and Yom Tov

hafrashas challah – separating a small piece from a large dough. The separated piece is then burned.

hakafos – the dancing with the Torah on Shemini Atzeres/Simchas Torah

hakaras hatov – being grateful

halachah [pl. halachos] – Jewish law

hasmadah – Diligence

Havdalah – the ceremony at the end of Shabbos and Yom Tov

hesped [pl. hespedim] – eulogies

kabbalas kahal – meeting the public

Kabbalas Shabbos – welcoming the Shabbos

kabbalos – mitzvos or stringencies a person undertakes

kallah – a bride

kasher – to make something kosher or to prepare it for use on Pesach

kibbud av va'eim – honoring parents

kiddush – (u.c.) the blessings over wine at the start of Shabbos and Yom Tov meals; a celebration Shabbos morning

kivrei tzaddikim – the graves of righteous people

kollel – a yeshivah for married men

korban – a sacrifice

Krias HaTorah – the public reading of the Torah

kuppah – box, esp. a box for coins

lashon hara – evil speech

lein – to read from the Torah

levayah – funeral

lichvod Shabbos kodesh – in honor of the holy Shabbos

L'shanah Tovah – a wish for a good year

Maariv – the evening prayer

maaser – $1/10$, when referring to money, it is the portion set aside for tzedakah

madrichah – counselor, guide

maggid shiur – a rebbi; someone who gives a Torah class

mah pitom? – "Why would you suddenly think that?" an exclamation

makolet – grocery, supermarket

mechalel Shabbos – breaking the rules of Shabbos

mechitzah – separation, usually between men and women

menachem avel – visiting a person during shivah after he/she lost a close relative

mesibah – get-together, party

mesirus nefesh – self-sacrifice

mevater – giving in to someone else

mezuzah [pl. mezuzos] – the parchment scroll with verses from the Torah hung on the doorpost

middos – character traits

middos tovos – good, proper character traits

midrashim – teachings of our sages

Minchah – the afternoon prayer

minhag – custom

minyan – a group of 10 men needed in order to say certain portions of davening

mishloach manos – gifts of food sent on Purim

morah – teacher

moshav – settlement, esp. an agricultural settlement

moshavnik – a person who lives on a moshav

motzi – to do a mitzvah for someone else

Mussaf – the special prayer added after Shacharis

neshamah – soul; person

netilas yadayim – washing hands for a religious reason

netz minyan – a minyan that davens the Shemoneh Esrei of Shacharis at sunrise

nichum aveilim – visiting a person during shivah after he/she lost a close relative

niftar – to pass away; the person who passed away

niggun [pl. niggunim] – songs

Nishmas Kol Chai – a prayer that expresses our thanks to Hashem

olam haba – the world to come

olam hazeh – this world

orchim – guests

parashah – the weekly Torah portion

parnassah – livelihood

perek – chapter

petirah – passing away

peyos – sidelocks; the hair at the side of a boy's head, at his ears

posek – a person who makes decisions in Jewish Law

posek hador – the greatest posek of the generation

rabbanit – rebbetzin; rabbi's wife

rav [pl. rabbanim] – rabbi

rebbi – teacher

refuah sheleimah – get-well wish

rosh – the head

ruach hakodesh – Divine inspiration

ruchniyus – spirituality

sandek – the one who holds the baby during the bris

savlanus – patience, forbearance

savta – grandmother

seder – order; a study period; (u.c.) the festival meal on the first night(s) of Pesach

sefer [pl. sefarim] – book, esp. a book with

Torah thoughts

Sefer Shemos – the second book of the Torah

sefer Torah – a Torah scroll

Sefiras HaOmer – the Counting of the Omer, the daily counting from the second night of Pesach until Shavuos

segulah – something with the spiritual ability to bring a person success

seudah – meal

seudah shelishis – the third Shabbos meal

Shabbos hi mi'liz'ok u'refuah krovah lavo – "On Shabbos we do not cry out. May a recovery come soon!" said on Shabbos when one gives recovery wishes to a sick person

Shacharis – the morning prayer

shadchanim – matchmakers

shanah tovah – a wish for a good new year

Shas – the entire Talmud

shekel [pl. shekalim] – the currency used in Israel

Shema, Shema Yisrael – the declaration of faith recited as part of prayers and before going to sleep

shemiras Shabbos – keeping the Shabbos

Shemoneh Esrei – the Amidah, the main part of the prayer service

Sheva Berachos – the seven blessings recited at meals for a week following a wedding; the meals at which the blessings are recited

shidduch – matching people for marriage

shiur [pl. shiurim] – class; measure

Shulchan Aruch – the Code of Jewish Law

Siddur – prayerbook

simchah – joy; a festive occasion

simchas hachaim – love of life

Simchas Torah – the day on which the completion of the yearly cycle of Torah reading is celebrated with dance and song

siyum – the completion of a portion of the Talmud; the meal celebrating that completion

sofer – scribe

s'machos – happy occasions and events

tallis – large, fringed prayer shawl worn during morning prayers

talmid – student

talmid chacham [pl. talmidei chachamim] – Torah scholar

tefillah [pl. tefillos] – prayer

tefillin – phylacteries

Tehillim – Psalms

teshuvah – repentance

tzaddik – righteous person

tzaros – problems, trouble

tzedakah – charity

tzidkus – piety

tznius – modesty

tzniusdik – modestly

Yehi Ratzon – a prayer recited when doing a mitzvah

yehi zichrah baruch – may her memory be a blessing

yeshivos gedolos – advanced yeshivos

yeshuah – salvation

yiras Shamayim – fear of Heaven

zechus [pl. zechuyos] – merit (n.)

zemiros – songs, esp. Shabbos songs

zocheh – merit (v.)

This volume is part of
THE ARTSCROLL SERIES®
an ongoing project of
translations, commentaries and expositions on
Scripture, Mishnah, Talmud, Midrash, Halachah,
liturgy, history, the classic Rabbinic writings,
biographies and thought.

For a brochure of current publications
visit your local Hebrew bookseller
or contact the publisher:

Mesorah Publications, ltd.

4401 Second Avenue
Brooklyn, New York 11232
(718) 921-9000
www.artscroll.com